DIALECT

OF THE

WEST RIDING

OF

YORKSHIRE

DIALECT

OF THE

WEST RIDING

OF

YORKSHIRE

A SHORT
HISTORY OF LEEDS AND OTHER TOWNS

BY

SAMUEL DYER, C.M.

with a new introduction by

STEWART F. SANDERSON

Director, Institute of Dialect and Folk Life Studies,
University of Leeds

———————

REPUBLISHED BY S. R. PUBLISHERS LTD. 1970
FIRST PUBLISHED BRIGHOUSE 1891

© S.R. Publishers Limited,
East Ardsley, Wakefield, Yorkshire

ISBN 0 85409 609 4

Reprinted in England by The Scolar Press Ltd.,
Menston, Yorkshire, U.K.

Introduction

There are many approaches to the study of dialects and many kinds of dialect books. Samuel Dyer's *Dialect of the West Riding of Yorkshire* is a typical and very good example of one of these approaches. It is learned, discursive and entertaining; it is also, let it be said at once, organised in a way which may prove baffling to the reader whose chief requirement is a regional dictionary or glossary on alphabetical lines. But if there appears to be little reason in Dyer's sequence of notes on dialect words there is rhyme in plenty, together with proverbs, anecdotes and phrases which richly illustrate local usage and wit. There are parallels, too, from other languages and from literary sources, while his notes on comparative philology are stimulating and, with only a few rare exceptions, reliable. His introductory essay, on the other hand, is out of date in some details: since Dyer's time our knowledge of pre-historic and dark age migrations and settlement, and of their ethnological and linguistic implications, has been considerably amplified and refined.

The picture of West Riding speech which is mirrored in Dyer's pages represents the usage of over a century ago; for although he does not list his sources of information as fully as would be thought appropriate today, it is clear that his compilation includes material from correspondents of mature years as well as his own reminiscences as a boy in the earlier half of the nineteenth century. His book is therefore of considerable historical importance.

It is interesting to compare his collections with those of the *Survey of English Dialects* a hundred years later, and to find — to cite only random examples — that the Scandinavian loan-words *lop*, *flay* and *laik* may still be heard for standard English *flea*, *scarecrow* and *play*; and to observe also that Yorkshiremen still proverbially 'addle their brass' if they haven't 'put Yorkshire on t'maister', while their children continue to chant traditional rhymes and play traditional games.

As a contribution to the history of West Riding life and speech Dyer's book remains a familiar landmark. It ought also to enccourage others to record similar material in our own times.

STEWART F. SANDERSON

DIALECT

OF THE

WEST RIDING

OF

YORKSHIRE:

A SHORT

HISTORY OF LEEDS AND OTHER TOWNS.

BY

SAMUEL DYER, C.M.,

EUSTON ROAD, LONDON.

———

"E mi in mezz' al magon."

———

BRIGHOUSE :
JOHN HARTLEY, PRINTER AND PUBLISHER.
—
1891.

NOTICE.

In this little book is an ethnological survey of the various races of men who have successively made incursions to this country, and the words they each have left behind, which have gone to build up the English we now speak. How words from one race have predominated in one locality, and become obsolete in another, thus forming what is termed dialect (not patois), is explained. Dialects may be trivialities to the purist, but thinking men consider them forces, racy of the soil, which will not readily die out. Many years have I occupied in studying various dialects, English and Continental; and in comparing them with that of Yorkshire, I find them all related more or less, being descended from the Aryan stock. Here are no fanciful derivations.

My thanks are due for valuable assistance to Clement Blackburn, Esq., of Brow Lee, near Brighouse, who is part owner of this book.

S. D.

107, EUSTON ROAD,
LONDON, N.W.

SUBSCRIBERS.

Lord Archbishop of Canterbury.
Lord Archbishop of York.
Lord Chief Justice Coleridge.
Earl of Wharncliffe.
Earl of Derby.
Clement Blackburn, Esq., Brow Lee, Brighouse.
Sam Blackburn, Esq., Phœnix Mill, Brighouse.
J. Stollard, Esq., Clay Cross.
G. Mills, Esq., Barnsley.
Æthelbert Binns, Esq., Wilsden.
Mr. R. Richardson, Euston Road.
Mr. John Dyer, Melegnano.
Sir Julian Goldsmid, Bart., M.P. Piccadilly.
Sir Morrell Mackenzie, Harley Street.
Sir Andrew Fairbairn, Bart.
Cavaliere Luigi Molteni, Naples.
Signora Sara Legnani.
Don Luigi Cusani, Chignolo.
Arthur Wilson, Esq., Tranby Croft.
E. J. Payne, Esq., Recorder of Chipping Wycombe.
R. Gilderdale Dyer, Secretary, United States Legation, Montevideo
Miss Fanny Dyer, Holloway.
T. J. Ashe, Esq., Montevideo.
Signor Arturo Dyer, Montagnana.
W. J. Young, Esq., G. N. R., Farringdon Road.
Señor Don Miguel Vucassovitch, Yaguaron.
Geo. Ibeson, Esq., Macclesfield.
J. Naylor, Esq., Brighouse.
Dr. Lawrie, Montevideo.
J. Sardesson, Esq., Calle Dayman, Montevideo.
H. Castle Ayre, Esq., Montevideo.
W. L. Poole, B.A., Reconquista.
John Sloane, Esq., Ibicui.
Wm. Shakespere, Esq., Rafaela.
Signor Tebaldo Garoni, Varese.

Professor Magrini, Collegio Longone.
Count Paolo Mantegazza, Milan.
W. F. Evelyn, Esq., Eynsford.
Mr. J, Murphy, Clerkenwell.
J. B. Macaulay, Esq., Maenclochog, Wales.
Miss Mary Cuthbert, Eltham.
Rev. Canon Jackson, Leeds.
Rev. Blomfield Jackson, Vicar of St. Bartholomew, Moorfields.
J. T. Barker, Esq., Burley View, Leeds.
J. O. Dayson, Esq., Secretary Mechanics' Institute, Leeds.
W E. Adams, Esq., Editor *Newcastle Weekly Chronicle*.
Wilson Barrett, Esq., Theatre Royal, Leeds.
Archibald Ramsden, Esq., Park Row, Leeds.
James Lattar, Esq., Knowsley.
G. M. Polini, Esq., New Olympic Theatre.
W. Lewis Hind, Esq., Sutton. Surrey.
Il Ministro Baccarini, Casamicciola, Ischia.
Mr. Samuel Coleman, Aden, Arabia.
Signor Lorenzo Bissone, Serodino, Rosario de Sa Fé.
R. R. Dees, Esq.,The Hall, Wallsend, Newcastle-on-Tyne.
J. C. Brocks, Esq., 14, Lovarne Place, Newcastle-on-Tyne.
Geo. Dyson, Esq., Marsden, near Huddersfield.
J. Horsfall Turner, Esq., F.R.H.S., Idel, near Bradford.
John Baldwin, Esq., Manager GasWorks, Honley, nr. Huddersfield.
James Sugden, Esq., Clifton, Brighouse.
Rev. Father Bernard Feeney, Aycuenaga.
Bertram Weall, Esq., Solicitor, Twickenham.
Dr. Faa di Bruno, Hatton Wall.
Count Gregor Schouvaloff, Monza.
Signor Tebaldo Garoni, Varese.
Rev. G. W. Garrod, Principal, Dioc. Tr. Coll., Ripon.
Signor Rubbattino, Tunis, Africa.
James Yates, Esq., Public Librarian, Leeds.
G. W. Usill, Esq., Civil Engineer, San Ramon.
R. Cranwell, Esq., Dashwood House.
G. Hamilton, Esq., Buenos Ayres.
Señor Don Venancio Solsona Flores, Soriano.
Lieutenant Jeeves, Sheffield.
Harry Job, Esq., Doncaster.
Keppel Blake, Esq., Isle of Wight.
George Baker, Esq., Birmingham.
Melville Geyelin, Esq., Kensington.
Signor Carlo Luini, Moltrasio.
Major Westropp.
Colonel Herbert Marryat.
Weldon Ashe, Esq., Calle Soriano.
El Ministro Bujareo, Aduana.
Mons. Albert Bazerque, Plaza Independencia.
Signor Carlo Servetti, Vasquez.

Mons. Bedouret, English Consulate.
Revd. Mr. Chamberlain, Missiones.
His Excellency Ernest Satow, English Minister, Montevideo.
Edward Field, Esq., Lightcliffe-road, Brighouse.
Rushton Turnoch, Esq., Lwchwy.
Signor E. Spreafico, Cassano d' Adda.
Signor Comm. Martorelli, Rome.
Signori Trombini, Melegnano.
Harry Eve, Esq., Barrister, Crouch End.
Rev. Peter Elkins, Long Eaton.
Rev. J. Perrett, Hook.
I. J. Hall, Esq., Highgate.
Mr. Geo. Watson, Hawnby.
Honourable General G. Muney, American Minister Plenipoten-
    tiary and Envoy Extraordinary to Uruguay.
W. J. Hill, Esq., U. S. Consul, Montevideo.
Percy Thursby, Esq., M.I.M.E., Chief Engineer, Ferro-carril del
    Oeste.
Captain Scott, Teddington
Sahib Korajaman Sen, B.A., Barrister, Calcutta.
H. Machin, Esq., Accountant, Burton Crescent.
Señor Daniel Muñoz, el Dia.
Chevalier Didier, Calle Lima.
Alfred Miles, Esq., Banker, Rosario.
J. McCrindle, Esq., Banker.
Edward Warnes, Esq., Leeds.
Herr Von Horn, Leipsig.
Herr Ludwig Getzt, Breslau.
T. Keay Tapling, Esq., M.P.
E. Witts, Esq., Architect.
J. Hill, Esq., Camaras.
Miss Kate Jones, South Kensington.
W. E. Morton, Esq., Calle, Columbia.
Very Rev. Canon Purcell, Child's Hill.
Rev. Canon Titcomb, Woking.
Mons. Lebraye, Paris.
    &c., &c.

RACES IN ENGLAND.

SAVAGE.
CAVE-MAN.
RIVERSIDE-MAN.
FLINT AGE.
BRONZE AGE.
IBERIAN.
GOIDELIC.
BRYTHONIC.
ANCIENT BRITON.
ROMAN, 45 B.C.
JUTE, 440 A.D.
NORSE.
SAXON, 477 A.D.
ANGLE, 600 A.D.
NORTHMAN.
DANE, 787 A.D.
NORMAN, 1066 A.D.
ENGLISH.

ERRATA.

Page 9, line 4, read Gnostic
" 12, " 30, " homogeneous
" 15, " 13, " Dano-Saxon
" 120, " 17, " Fine.

PROEM.

DEMOGRAPHY will not permit me to make deep scrutiny into the origin of man, whether as from a protoplasmic, sarcode germ, a jelly, bathybius monad; or, as a sublimer agnostic philosophy once taught, that the vital principle emanated (a bright effluence, a ray of light) from the grand pleroma of light, "offspring of heaven, first-born," and that the ethereal essence evolving the sensibility of the visual organ will in the far future be re-gathered into a beautiful beam, to be re-absorbed into "the Father of all lights." This we *do* know, in spite of agnosticism—that man is. Now, as we do not wish to parvify humanity, we shall merely say :—

The earth revolves on its axis eastward. Man in his struggle for existence migrates westward.* Successive hordes have swept onwards, following the setting sun, ages before the Aryan from India rolled its waves of Kelt, Teuton and Slav to overflow the sea-board of Europe.

In Scandinavia traces of two distinct races have been found before the arrival of the true Swea.

The Norwegian Lapps nowadays preserve their uncivilised and nomadic manner of life : they are now what they were millions of years ago. There is a well-founded belief that in pre-historic times this curious people inhabited

---

* The Chinese, however, wandered eastward ; one other instance is found in Gen. iv, 16. Curiously enough Sir Walter Scott sinks the sun in the east (*Antiquary*, ch. 7).

Denmark, that the Kjokkenmöddings are their work, and that the dark-complexioned folk whom we now and then see among the fair-haired Scandinavians exhibit traces of an ancestry more ancient than the Aryans. But the invasion of the latter gradually drove them backwards until they were confined to the northern part of the peninsula. About Trondhjem and Oestersund are found ancient tombs, midding-kitchens and places of worship, and names of Lappish origin. Here also the Lapps, though nominally converts to Christianity, retain, as do the Lutheran Greenlanders of the present day, some of their Pagan customs, whereas farther south they are good members of the new faith, and have changed even in type.

Will you examine critically the anthropology and the demography of the dual races in any country of Europe? In Ireland it is said a people called the Firbolg* lived prior to the Milesian who preceded the Erse. In Britain, from the contents of barrows, ethnologists have come to the conclusion that a set of men existed pre-historically anterior to the Ancient Briton. It has long been recognised that the Celts of these islands may be divided into two great branches, the one represented by the Irish and the Scotch Islanders, and the other by the Welsh. The former division is designated by modern scholars the Goidelic, and the latter the Brythonic. That the Goidels were the first to come to Britain there is no doubt, and the fact is universally admitted. They drove the Ibernians, whom they found in the island, to the west and north, and were in turn driven in the same direction by their Brythonic successors. It was till lately supposed that at the time of the Roman invasion the Goidels had entirely disappeared as a separate race from Southern Britain, and were only to be found north of the Forth and Clyde. There is, however, abundant evidence to show that this is a mistake, and that even after the departure of the Romans, a considerable part of Wales, and probably also of Cornwall, was of Goidelic blood. Numerous inscribed stones have been found in Wales, the writing on which is in a peculiar character known as the Ogham. These inscriptions have been deciphered by means of a key

---

* Of the dolichocephalic skull.

contained in old Irish manuscripts, and the Celtic language in which they are written belongs clearly to the Goidelic division of the linguistic family. There is, therefore, good ground for believing that at the beginning of the Christian era, large districts in the western portion of the island were inhabited by tribes of Goidelic origin, to some extent, mingled with an earlier Ibernian population. The Brythons occupied the eastern and central parts, and appear to have extended north as far as the Forth and Clyde. There was a marked distinction in many ways between the two races. The Goidels were much less advanced in civilisation than the Brythons, though doubtless much above their Ibernian predecessors. The Brythonic tribes carried on a considerable commerce with the Continent; some of them had a regular coinage stamped and lettered, while the Goidels had but little foreign trade, and used only metal bars and rings in exchange. The physical features of the two branches of the Celtic race were not very different. Both were tall and light-haired, in opposition to the short and dark-haired Ibernians. The Brythons certainly were not mere savages as regards their dress. The name is said to mean clothed, and they wore cloaks of striped plaid-cloth. Some of the Goidels may have done the same, but others dressed themselves in skins like the Ibernians. And in North Spain and South France there are two isolated generations existing now, imagined to be of the Tauranian family of the cyclocephalic skull, and are respectively called Basque and Escuara. The Spaniards name theirs Gallegos,* and the French theirs Euscaldures, They are thought to be descendants of the Iberi, a tribe of dark-haired, short-legged men with high cheek bones, who seized both sides of the Pyrenees long before the Visigoth invaded Spain, or the Francs France. With regard to the other peoples passed away, their existence is surmised and partly known from the contents of barrows, such as implements of offence and defence; from their canoes, or Einbaums as the Germans term them, and Dug-outs as they have been named across the Atlantic, being a log or trunk of a tree chipped out with flints or burnt out with fire when man had progressed so far as to be able to evolve *heat* by

---

* Because of their being in the West of Spain (see No. 17).

friction, a proceeding which throws much *light* on their manner of life, food, and struggles ; as well as from the study of the midding-heaps in Norway and their lacustrine villages in Switzerland. Where skeletons have been found, craniology shews them to have been of a totally different type of humanity from the existing European. Later on advanced tribes have been traced in Ireland, through a kind of short-hand writing called oghams, something like the runes of the Scandinavians or the arrow-heads of Ninevah.

In Wales at the present day you may see two distinct types of men, say a (present) pre-historic Iber and an (modern) Ancient Briton. Nature is careless of the species, but provident of the type. It wants no Danish Ibsen to prove heredity as an iron law. We are all aware of the retreating brow of a Bourbon or the thick lip of a Hapsburg.

And it might have been supposed that the blending of various races would have obliterated the general type ; but the matriarchal principle is everlastingly evolved through the anabolic and katabolic energies of an archaic race In all countries, from time immemorial, there has been a conflict of higher white and lower coloured stock. Even specifically there may be found one of a family departing from the other members in feature, hair, gesture, and stature : with a little retrospective consideration it is traceable to a maternal ancestor. How often, on the bed of death, the bystanders remark " How like his grandmother : though we never noticed it before." Tennyson says this.

Recent researches have shewn that the Australian Aborigines are not a homogenous stirp of black fellows, but among them are also found clear traces of a struggle between higher and lower races. In Italy, the land of the descendants of Rome—black-haired, bright-eyed, swarthy-skinned—you may meet with a beautiful blonde, *una bella bionda*, light-haired, blue-eyed, diaphanous-skinned, most " divinely fair." Is it not the re-appearance of the old Goth who overran the Imperial City, or the Longbeard who seized upon the Euganean plains of Lombardy ?

Coming to historic times ; the Aryan sent out branches : Keltic, Pelasgic, Teutonic, and Sclavonic. The Teutonic spread out into two ramifications, the Ancient British and Ancient Irish ; where these settled the former originated the Welsh, the French Gaul, and the Armoric Breton ; and the latter Manx, Gaelic (Highland Scotch), and Erse. The Welsh have left us words for many physical objects, for the aspects of nature, rivers flowing, winds blowing, hills and dales, glens and vales, islands and dry land, lakes and mountains, streams and fountains; but, with the exception of about seventy words more, for common things, they have bequeated us nothing else, neither influence of race character nor signs of political power, because when driven from their home by the Saxon they took away with them their language and whatever Latin they had learnt from the Romans.

The Romans during their stay in Britain never succeeded entirely in superseding the language of the old Celt ; and many words they left in the island were cut out by the ferocity of the short-sworded Saxon. Indeed the small number of present English words derived from Latin, and which are chiefly ecclesiastical terms, were introduced several hundred years later by the Saxon monks, and the mass of Latin derivatives for terms of science were not incorporated into our tongue until a race of native philosophical writers arose —the 15th and 16th centuries. An opinion is prevalent that the Latin was never a spoken language in this island, except among the Roman Legions, and a few Britons who by their force of genius pushed themselves into the policy of their conquerors : for the Romans intentionally taught them little, excluded them from all offices, took their best young men to fill up their foreign legions, and used the rest as beasts of burden ; or if they taught them at all it was on Shakespere's principle that

> Heaven doth with us as we with torches do,
> Not light them for themselves.—*Measure for Measure.*

and when they abandoned this Island they left the Britons so deplorably ignorant, even in the art of war, Rome's great characteristic, that these were compelled to call in a barbarous horde to assist them against another barbarous horde. On the other hand the Romans, the most majestic people of antiquity, must have conferred a certain amount of civilisation,

as they did on the inhabitants of other conquered provinces;
but commensurate with the time they stayed here, and
the counteracting influence of incursive rude tribes. The
population of the towns which formed the important body of
the inhabitants, says another great thinker, and at the close
of the empire the rest of the people also, talked Latin, as in
the other provinces of the empire ; and if our Teutons from
the north had never come, the people of the Island would
have been a people talking a Roman dialect, as are French,
Spanish, Portuguese, Roumanian, Provençal and Italian.
Tindal (of the Polymetic) says " that Agricola (governor of
Britain under Vespasian), seeing that our ancestors were a
rough, barbarous, valiant and restless people, ever ready to
rebel, resolved to soften their ferocity by introducing the Roman
language, arts and customs among them ; this we learn from
his son-in-law, Tacitus, in his life of Agricola." Our ancient
Britons wisely fell into the customs of the conquerors,
adopted their school education, and studied their language.
It seems, by a passage in Juvenal (Sat. xv, v. 112) that fifty
years after, the love of the Roman customs and language
had so far prevailed that the British lawyers pleaded in
Latin, as years after the English did in Norman-French—
after the conquest.   This law-Latin and Norman-French
still survives in many legal terms.   I am persuaded that Latin
was used to some extent in our towns, even down to a later
date, in the Anglo-Saxon period, than many suppose. The
Celtic tribes (Ancient Britons), retiring before the Saxon,
settled in Wales, Cornwall, and (to a smaller extent) in
Lancashire and Cumberland, while the Breton had already
peopled Armorica, giving it the name of Brittany.* The
Saxon power of the language began to be developed,
and the inherent elements for creating new words were
fully evolved from its own stores, like the old Greek and
the modern German. It was a most copious tongue, full
of grammatical inflections, and was fraught with a nervous

---

* Our empire is called " Great Britain " in distinction to this
Brittany. Cockneys, however, think it in distinction to Little Britain,
near St. Martin's-le-Grand, London. Since our Colonies have been
so multiplied Hepworth Dixon hit upon a noble phrase—Greater
Britain—to particularise the mighty empire on which the sun never
sets.

energy, and in spite of Horace Walpole's assertion* that there "never did exist a more barbarous jargon than the dialect (?) still venerated by antiquaries and called Saxon," it is now acknowledged that it was hardy and happy, joining together after a most eloquent manner "sundry words of every kind of speech." It was peculiarly rich in synonyms.

Such was the language of the Saxons in England, when another rude tribe rushed over the country and pushed it back into ignorance and mental darkness. The Danes spoke a dialect not differing much from that of the Saxons. These cruel struggles between two related Teutonic tribes ceased in the course of time, and their sister dialects became blended into one tongue. A new idiom, the Dana-Saxon, might have arisen on the old ruins if it had been permitted ; but by the time the two races became friendly and their dialectic differences assimilated, another tribe of the Scandinavian hordes overran the country, bringing with them their Norman-French. This Norman-French was not entirely their own language, but the one they had combined with that adopted from the French race they conquered when they seized on Neustria. It is to the mixture of these two languages (Saxon and Norman-French) on our English soil, that our tongue possesses that duality of words which renders it so musical and expressive. Most words for the common purposes of life are Anglo-Saxon ; while terms for chivalry, the chase, and the higher state of the nobles are Norman-French. At no period, however, did one intruding language entirely annihilate its predecessor. All mingled harmoniously. However, in some localities certain words were retained, others dropped; some words acquired a different shade of meaning,† and so

---

* *Walpole's Historic Doubts*, p. 10.

† Something similar is found in the Romance languages, where, *e.g.*,

Spanish.	*Italian.*	*French.*
Salir, to get out	Salire, to go up	Salir, to dirty
Sentir, to feel	Sentire, to hear	Sentir, to smell

As Whately in his *Logic* points out : Hypostasis (Greek), substantia (Lat.), understanding (Eng.), sottinteso (It.), sousentre (Fr.), unterstehen (Germ.) are exact in etymology, and yet widely different in meaning. There is Lance's little joke of his staff *understanding* him, because, says he, "it *stands under* me" (*Two Gentlemen of Verona*, Skakespere).

we may account for dialects. For instance, speculative
Jonathan receiving his English from the Pilgrim Fathers
resembles more than we do the Englishman of the 16th
century, even to the Puritanical droning through the nose.
I do not consider a dialect as a *patois* or a variety of the
vernacular, otherwise one may term it a brogue. To me it
is a language, because many of its words have a different
origin from the equivalents in the cognate tongue : others
possess an older form. Why? You do not consider
French a dialect of the Italian because there are thousands
of words in common? For myself, I cherish the Doric
speech of the canny Scot, the trilled burr of Newcastle, the
open vowel of Norfolk, the *thic* of Dorset, and the flat
buzz of my " Vrend fro' Zomerzetzher." But above all,
to me is dear the broad sound heard in the West Riding.
And what of the hardy Norseman, whose fair-faced, golden-
haired, light-blue-eyed, ferocious sires of yore, under their
Vikings bold, swooped in their dragon ships out of
fjords of Gamle Norge across the stormy sea, down on
the coasts of Britain, the Danelagh, the Angle-land, the
Saxon-land ; and along the shores of Gaul and Spain as
Northman, soon to re-appear as Norman. After such
intractable opponents the feeble folk of southern lands were
an easy prey, and the dragon ships became a terror to the
shores and river banks of Western Europe, and even of the
Mediterranean. This Norman by-and-bye does mocking
homage to a French king at Rouen, and afterwards teaches
a nobler courtesy to the chivalry of France, when the beauty
and charm of Norman ladies held captive the Princes of
Europe, when Norman valour and genius, after planting a
rich, if rude, literature in the snows of Iceland, left their
traces in relics of noble architecture and manifold beauty
along the valley of the Seine, built up the kingdom of the
two Sicilies, and grafted on the sluggish and besotted Anglo-
Saxon stem the elegant energy which blossomed forth in
the Chaucers and Shakspeares, the Miltons and Byrons, the
Drakes and Nelsons. This is a brilliant romance, as any in
history.

Normandy even now is proverbially *Le pays de sapience.*
We feel a proud wonder at the grand progress our age has

made during the last ninety years, with the aid of many inventions; but what of the contrast between the warrior of the dragon ships, who came south with Rolf (or Rollo), and startled the people of Jumièges some time early in the 10th century, and the gallant host assembled in 1066 around William from all parts of Europe by the blessing of the Pope, when the duke awaited at St. Valery a fair breeze to carry him across to Hastings. The hundred years of Norman progress, with only strong hearts to will and hands to hew the way, may well compare with the years of modern progress, though the telegraph and the steam engine, with a train of conquered forces of nature, have helped it. We have invented much, and discovered more, in modern days, but it may be doubted if our architects of the present time excel those of Normandy; if the examination schools of Oxford present any fairer enthusiasm for learning than did the Abbey of Bec under Lanfranc; if our civilisation is adequate to produce a stronger will or a keener intellect than that of the stern Conqueror, pious and just withal, who dug so deep the foundations of England's greatness.

W O R D S .

AFTER the retirement of the Romans from this island the invading immigrants were the Jutes, Saxons, Danes and Angles, who settled in the following manner: the Jutes seized Kent, the Isle of Wight, and a part of the mainland; the Saxons had all those parts that have now the suffix "sex," as Essex, Sussex, Middlesex, and (the obsolete name) Wessex; and the Angles took possession of that tract of the north that has the present terminations "land," "shire," and "folk," as Suffolk, Yorkshire, Northumberland, &c. These last afterwards gave the name to the whole island. There is an Anglen at this present time in Schleswig-Holstein; and strange to say, Holbeck, near Leeds, is found in Yorkshire as well as in that province of Denmark;* and a most marked resemblance even now is observed between the Yorkshire dialect, the Frisian and the Schleswig-Holsteiner. It may be noted that the Saxons introduced into their settlements the division of counties into hundreds, the Jutes into lathes, one county into rapes, and the Angles into wapentakes. Although the Angles gave a name to our island, England—Inglaterra (Spanish), Angleterre (French), Inghilterra (Italian)—to the Welsh, Irish, and Highlanders we are still Sassenach. About the year 800 A.D. the Danes poured in their piratical hordes, but it was not till 1017 A.D. that they effected a settlement in the northern counties on the eastern coast. It is to these Angles and Danes

---

* Holbeck is found in Yorks., Notts., and Lincolnshire; in Schleswig, as well as in French Flanders: Hollebeque. It is Norse, and means narrow stream.

that many of the Yorkshirisms are to be traced, as well as
to the fact that certain words clung to certain counties, while
they became obsolete in others.   Dialects are not to be
considered corruptions of a language, but as varieties less
favoured than the principal tongue of the country.   If by
fortuitous circumstances the Court had been established at
Oldham instead of at London, there is every philological
reason to believe that the racy dialect of Tim Bobbin would
have become the English language.   Again, many Yorkshire words still linger in the old writers ; and as no two
nations have the same wants—words being invented to
express those ·wants—it follows that in dialects are often
found words that have no exact equivalents in the vernacular: consequently it sometimes occurs that a country is
richer in its provincialisms.   It is my purpose to give
instances of these, with quotations from various authors,
and to catalogue a few of the most marked words of my
own county which differ materially from the metropolitan.

Of the various dialects in England, it must be borne in
mind that the northern counties retain many words now
obsolete in current English : these words are of the genuine
Teutonic stock.   The pronunciation may seem rough and
harsh, but is the same as that used by our forefathers ;
consequently it must not be considered barbarous.   The
other counties of England differ from the vernacular by a
depraved pronunciation.   However, we must except the
East-Anglian counties, because of the Danes making a
settlement in Norfolk and Suffolk ; besides, in King John's
time, a fleet of sixty thousand soldiers from Brittany and
Flanders, being wrecked on the coast, remained in these
counties (vide Dr. Brown, of *Urn Burial* memory) ; and
in consequence of the Revocation of the Edict of Nantes
many Huguenot French and Flemish settled near Norwich
—some at Spitalfields, near London.   The real dialects of
England, therefore, are : Yorkshire, Lancashire and Cumberland, Norfolk and Suffolk.   The Northumbrian may be
considered Lowland Scotch.   Yorkshire being so large in
extent, it will be found that the Ridings differ considerably
in their words ; and thus a native of Halifax will have many
words not in use at Stokesley.   If Lancashire owes much
to the Welsh element, Yorkshire does to the Jutes and

Danes. All the sea coast of Yorkshire, Durham and Northumberland, was called at one time the Danelagh. An old writer (Trevisa), in his translation of Higden's *Polychronicon* (A.D. 1387), says :—" All the langage of the Northumbers and specialliche at York is so sharpe, slitting, and frotynge and unschape that we southern men may that langage unnethe understonde. I trow that it is bycause that they beethe nigh to strange men and nations that speketh strongliche, and also bycause that the kings of Englonde woneth always far from that cuntry." Trevisa's language seems to me as " sharpe and slitting " as the one he writes about. It is much the same as a poem with an illustration. However, it characterises the Yorkshire dialect well, and the last reason which he gives for this sharpness is true. The dialect of the Angles was broader and harsher than that of the Saxons and of the Jutes, and was known by the later name Danna-Saxon, the dialect of the Saxons being called Anglo-Saxon.

Agglomeration of the verb and pronoun is common in the Yorkshire dialect, instances of which are given in the following tetralogue :—

Priest (loq.) : Wilt thou have this woman ? &c.
Man (rather deaf) : Wot dun him say, lass ?
Woman : He says, witta homma ?
Friend (explaining) : He says, witta hover?
Man (enthusiastic) : Willa hotha? Ay, mun. A com here ta hotha. (Turning to the priest) : Ye're reight, maister ; morry on.

Here *homma, hover, hotha,* signify *have me, have her,* and *have thee ;* and *witta, willa,* mean *wilt thou, will I.* This process works through all languages, and therefore no wonder its effects should be appreciated in dialects. In the Anglo-Saxon literature *wit,* or *we two, git,* or *ye two,* are instances sufficient for my purpose. Chaucer wrote *shaltow* for *shalt thou, siestow* for *sayest thou, gowe* for *go we, so theek* for *so thee ich* or *so thrive I, froye* for *from you, nis* for *is not, noulde* for *would not.* Even the modern *wilt* and *shalt* are instances where the verb and pronoun coalesce to form verbal person : indeed all the inflexions of words are modifications of annexed pronouns.—See Tooke's *Div. of Parley,* Latham's *Eng. Gram.* and *Vestiges of Creation.* Amongst many of the languages of the Indians this law goes

on until sometimes not only the pronouns are absorbed into
the principal word, but even adjectives. This system has
been aptly termed Polysynthetic. As an illustration,
Kuligatschis (in the Delaware-Indian dialect) is the agglomeration of *Ke* the pronoun, *Uli* part of *wulet* (pretty),
Gat part of *wichgat* (paw), *Schis* a diminutive term of
endearment : so that *Kuligatschis* is *Ke-wulet-wichgat-schis*,
Give me your pretty little paw. In Italian such phrases as
Give me some of them, *Speak to him about it*, are by this
agglutination, *Datemene*, *Parlategliene*. In the Milanese
dialect *damm* is for *date à me*, *dill* for *dite à lui*, *meuvem* for
io muovo, &c. In East Anglia some one remarked "When
I was a boy, my father would never have said 'Go and
plough,' but 'Gowe,' meaning not Go you, but Go we, as
he would have helped." The Anglo-Saxon had a dual like
the old Greek :

> Nom. wit, we two.
> Gen. uncer, of us two.
> Dat. unc, to us two.

In an old German Forma (date 685) I met with this
expression, "Forsachistu diabolæ? Gelobistu in Got;"
and the opening line of the *Form of Trial* by the terrible
Vehme Gericht (circa 1220) is "Herr Greve met Orlove,"
i.e., Sir Count, with your leave. The agglomeration is here
plainly seen. By the way, this Orlove is interesting, appearing in later German Urlub, then Urlaub ; and as a phrase
"auf urlaub" gives us by a second amalgamation "fur-
lough." The Dutch have the same error, "Verlof." To
resume : In Icelandic the definite article follows the noun,
and unites with it as one word, to form gender, number,
and person. This is also the case in Danish, Swedish, and
Norwegian, but the traces of the added part are almost
hidden. In the Scandinavian there was coalition of the
reflective pronoun and the verb in certain conditions of the
verb. In Welsh the verb and pronoun agglutinate to form
number and person, but as prefixes. In Somersetshire
you will meet with *Cham* for *I am*, *Chould* for *I would*, &c.
In Icelandic occur *cutna* for *cut not*, and in Scotch *winna*,
munna, *shanna*, *canna*. A learned professor asserts this law
to be peculiar to the old poetical dialect of Scandinavia
only; but from the few examples adduced it is by inference

a law that governs the whole circle of tongues ; and the verbs were made to express time, person, manner, by inflectional declensions. Afterwards a second step, a verbal attrition has rubbed off the cumbersome corner of cases, and by a happy substitution of connecting words has conduced to that simplicity of expression so remarkable in the modern languages, in which the Yorkshire dialect has its share.

(1.) BRAT (Anglo-Saxon), a coarse apron. In Yorkshire, " brat " is a child, probably because nursed in the apron, hence to breed, and that which is bred, viz., a brood. Gascoigne writes, " Oh, Abraham's brats, oh brood of blessed seed." Here it is clear that a connection exists between brat and brood ; and it may also be remarked that *brat* had not with the old writers the contemptuous tone it now possesses. In Scott's *Fair Maid of Perth*, c. 13, there is " brattach," which he explains, a standard of coarse cloth. Chaucer writes " bratt," which my friend Mr. Wright, F.S.A., defines " a coarse mantle." The verb to brood is to think deeply and long, but the primary meaning was to *idea*, to conceive ; and it is in this sense that Milton says in reference to the creation,

> His brooding wings the Spirit of God outspread,
> And vital virtue infused and vital warmth
> Throughout the fluid mass.—*Paradise Lost*, book vii.

(2.) BARN (A. Saxon), bairn (Scotch), a child, from " born," just as in Latin, natus means both " born " and " a child." In the same way puiné (French), whence our " puny," and aîné (French), refer to the youngest and the eldest born. The Norwegian shows at once that *barn* means a child because it is *born*, for barn is singular and bjorn is plural. Ulphilas translates " the damsel is not dead, but sleepeth," by "that a barn ni gadauthnoda, ac slepith ;" and " the children's bread," by " hlaib barne." Shakespeare quibbles on the double meaning of barn : a stable, a child. " Then if your husband have stables enough, you'll see he shall lack no barns."—*Much Ado*, iii., 4. " A very pretty barn."— *Winter's Tale*, iii., 3. " That gets the bairn's bread."—*Scotch Song*. The Anglo-Saxon version of John i., 12, has " Godes bairn " for " the sons of

God;" and in the ballad of *Valentine and Orsin* there
is, "a bairn of high degree." "A byrd hav I brought to
my barne."—*Towneley Myst.*, 118. "A maydn a barn shall
bere," (*Towneley Myst.*, 158,) is Isaiah's "Behold a virgin
shall conceive." In Danish, barndom is childhood, spædt
barn is a baby, and barnebarn is a grandson: this last is far
more expressive of its meaning than our hybrid of English
and French. Bare, signifying uncovered (bar in Anglo-
Saxon), is also derivable from to bear, for a reason see Job
i., 21. Barren is also a cognate, either as meaning bare of
children, or not bearing. In the Penitential of Egbert,
Archbishop of York, the opening words are: "Gif hwalc
Cristen man his agen Bearn, oththe his nehstan mæg
with anigum wurthe sylle, næbbe he nanne gemanan mid
Cristenum mannum," which may be rendered, "If each
Christian man sell for a price his own child or his nearest
relation, he shall not have fellowship with Christian men."
"But they had long ceased to burn farms, sack convents,
torture monks for gold, and slay every human being they
met, in mere Berserker lust of blood. No *Barnakill* could
now earn his nickname by entreating his comrades, as they
tossed the children on their spear points to 'Na kill the *barns.*'
Gradually they had settled down on the land, intermarried
with the Angles and Saxons, and colonised all England
north and east of Watling Street (a rough line from London
to Chester), as far as the Tees. Gradually they had deserted
Thor and Odin for 'the white Christ ;' had their own priests
and bishops, and built their own minsters."—Kingsley's
Hereward the Wake.

(3.) BARM (Lancashire dialect) is a bosom cloth or apron.
"Thus day by day this child began to cry till in its fadres
barm adown it lay."—Chaucer's *Monkes Tale,* 15925. "A
barm-clothe eke as white as morwe milk."—Chaucer's
Millers Tale. When the apron is made of leather it is
called a barm-skin. "He had his knockus (knuckles) lapt
in his barm-skin."—(Tim Bobbin.) "Barm," meaning
yeast, from bearma (A. Saxon), or perhaps from beerheim
(German) ; over-beer is another word altogether. "To go
to the barm-kin high."—Ballad of *Lord Soulis.* See No.
136.

(4.) BOKEN (by the elision of L) is another form of belch ; and expresses eructation, the tendency to vomit— *bealcan*. (Anglo-Saxon.) Sometimes written belk, the root of the word is belly, as yolk and yellow are connected "They never leave belking till it be up."—Gosson's *School of Abuse* (temp.1579.) In English it used to mean liquor : "Porters would no longer be drunk with belch.—*Dennis*. See No. 97.

(5.) FLAY (Yorkshire), to frighten; flay-craw, a scarecrow. Connected with fray (afraid) and éffrayer (French) to frighten; it is an instance where *r* is displaced by *l*, of which there are many examples in all languages. The change of *r* to *l* is termed lallation. The Sandwich Islanders call their capital Honolulu, and it is spelt Honoruru. The Chinaman will say "Very well, Englishman lich. Me pigeon olanges." —his jargon meaning: "Very well; you are rich. I will do business with you in oranges." "It spak right howe : My name is Death. But be na *fleyd*."—Burns' *Dr. Hornbook*. "I'm *flay'd* to death" means I'm very frightened, and is no more to be taken literally than the Irishman's "kilt entirely," or "For thy sake are we killed all day long," (*Psalm* xliv., 22.) or the Latin *perimo*, to kill thoroughly.

(6.) CLICK, another form of clutch, as make of match, bake of batch. A Yorkshireman will say "Click ho'd, mun," for catch hold, and the Milanese say "Tacca ti tacc." In Jutland it is "Klække ved."

(7.) DAWKIN, used only in the West Riding, is an idle fellow, as seen in the saying "Better a dule for a wife than a dawkin," meaning better a devil for a wife than a lazy slut. In Lancashire, slunt (from the Danish) means the same.

(8.) GAWK is the left hand, and gawky is awkward ; auke (A. Saxon) is left handed. Some old writers use *aukely* for *awkwardly*, and many grammarians doubt whether it ought not to be *awkard*. Dryden writes it so, and in Yorkshire it is always so pronounced. The right hand, from being always in use, acquires a dexterity not possessed by the left. Accordingly we find that all derivatives of words for the right hand indicate expertness. Dextra (Latin), the right hand, gives us dexterity, &c., as sinistra (Latin), the left

hand, gives us sinistrous. So the left hand in Italian
manca, in Provençal *man seneca*, have bad qualities referring
to the mind; while in Spanish izquierdo and derecho mean
left and right, yet for left-handed it is zurdo, and for
awkward they make use of the paraphrastic expression *poco
diestro*. In Buenos Ayres and Montevideo they have a word,
half Indian and half-Spanish, maturrango, for an awkward
fellow. Of course this sinister means ominous; but writers
often use it in its legitimate sense. " In his sinister hand
.   .   .   he placed a mighty mug of potent ale."—
Dryden. The French gauche (left hand) gives them a
noun gaucherie, awkwardness; and the German links (left
hand) creates linkish, which has the same meaning as the
Yorkshire gawky. In the district of Todmorden, I several
times heard old residents speak of a left-handed person as
being key-dawled. "Dawl," or " dall," hand, is derived
from the Celtic d'lamh, pronounced dlav. We get it in
significant phrases like ' Keep thy dawls eawt o' that !"
" Keep thy dawls to thysel !"   " We want nooan o' his
dawls i' this deeal !"   " Key-dawl," or "key-dall," left-
handed. This very peculiar and local expression is an am-
plification of " dall." " Cith " (pronounced " kith," nearly
like " kidth "), left, and " d'lamh," pronounced " lav," hand;
cith-lamh, pronounced " kidth-lav," left-handed. The expression is used at present amongst Highlanders. There
was on Order of Fools instituted by Count Adolphus of
Cleves, 1381, which bore the name of " D'Order van't
Geeken Gesellschap;" this is the original of gawk; and in
corroboration it is worthy of notice that the Scotch April-
gowk is our April-fool. I am aware that this gowk is a
cuckoo, in Anglo-Saxon geac; but the cuckoo is not the
only bird whose name has become synonymous with fool,
and other vituperative words : *ex. gr.*, booby, gull, &c.
A boy may be a big *goose*, but a girl is a little *duck*.

(9.) BLACK-CLOCK is the black-beetle. The Scandinavian
klúka means a beetle. In an old poem, *Christ's Kirk on
the Green*, generally attributed to James I. of Scotland (A.D.
1437), there occurs "counted him not twa clocks;" and
Tennyson, in his *Northern Farmer*, writes, " An 'eerd a
bumming away like a buzzard-clock o'er my yead ;" this

means, and heard a buzzing over my head like a cock-chafer.   In the *Pogmoor Almanac or Bairnsley Folks' Annual* there was a pictorial joke of a black-clock, and under it was written " Sable Chronometer."

(10.) ABIDE (Yorkshire), to bear or suffer.   They say, for instance, " I can't abide him," meaning I cannot endure him.   " Nor can I abide any tongue that will prattle and prate against reason."—Ballad of *Plain Dealing Man.*

> For God's sake hide it.
> It is so ugly, we may not abide it.
> —Drayton's *Moon Calf.*

" Was no barne that could her byde."—*Felon Sow of Rokeby* (A.D. 1609).   It is plain that this meaning of the word has arisen from the primary meaning : for what one cannot abide (endure), is what one cannot abide (stay near).   " Commonly we say a judgment falls upon a man for something in them we cannot *abide.*"   " Henry IV. of France once said he was killed for his wenching, another said he was killed for turning his religion.   ' No,' says King James (who could not *abide* fighting), ' he was killed for permitting duels in his kingdom.' "—*Selden's Table-Talk*, Article on " Judgments."   " So it falls out in that which is the great pleasure of some men, tobacco, at first they could not *abide* it, and now they cannot do without it."—*Selden's Table-Talk*, Article on " Pleasure."

> I cannot *bide* Sir Baby.
> —Tennyson's *Idylls :* " Pelleas."

> Oh, young knight,
> Hath the great heart of knighthood in thee failed,
> So far thou canst not *bide* a fall from him.—*Ibid.*

> Ah me ! they little know
> How dearly I *abide* that boast.
> —Milton's *Paradise Lost*, iv, 86.

' And this I heard, that the king's daughter cannot *abide* him, and would as lief marry a seal.'

' One may pick a fair quarrel with him nevertheless.'

' Then you must *bide* such a buffet as you never *abode* before. They say his arm has seven men's strength ; and whosoever visits him, he challenges to give and take a blow : but no man that has taken a blow as yet has ever needed another.'

' Hereward will have need of his magic headpiece, if he tries that adventure,' quoth another.

'Ay,' retorted the first speaker, 'but the helmet may stand the rap well enough, and yet the brains inside be the worse.'

'Not a doubt. I knew a man once, who was so strong that he would shake a nut till the kernel went to powder, and yet never break the shell.'

'That is a lie !' quoth Hereward. And so it was, and told purposely to make him expose himself.—*Hereward*, xiii.

(11.) CUDDLE (a Yorkshire word), to hug warmly to the breast, from Cadail (Celtic), meaning sleep. "They cuddled close all night."—Somerville's *Fables*, xi. This Celtic word gives us the proper name Cadell, also to coddle and mollycoddle. "It was made a *sine qua non* that the plants were grown out of doors all the year round, and not *coddled* into 'perfection' under the protecting influence of a glass structure."—*The Times*. Cod, in Old English, was a pillow or bag, and it is connected with peascod; while in Middlesex codder is a pea gatherer, and the London slang, to cod, is to hoodwink : you see the hood, pillow or bag ? The cud (of a cow) is also akin to this cuddle, and so is the sailor's quid. "In Kent, a cow is said to chew her *quid*, so that cud and quid are the same."—*Pegge*. The Latin Professor, seeing a student's cheek distended, asked "Quid est ?" to which the student replied "Quid of tobacco, est !" Quid rides ? Douglas Jerrold, in his inimitable *Curtain Lectures*, had such idea in his mind when he named his hero Job Caudle. Craig thinks caudle derived from *chadeau* (French), something warmed ; and he gives an explanation—gruel and ale, spice and sugar mixed, which shows how plausible philologists can be in their derivations, and yet be wrong. "He gave her rich caudle."—Poem called the *Death of Queen Jane*, 1537. "Caudle thy morning toast."—*Shakespeare*. "One single sniff at Charlotte's caudle-cup."—*Warton*. "Most of them are begotte overnight in tobacco smoke and muldsacke, and uttered and delivered to the world's presse by the helpe and midwifery of a *caudle* the next morning."—*John Melton*, 1607 ("a five-fold politician"). "But wan't she as good to cuddle and kiss as a lass as an't nowt."—Tennyson's *Northern Farmer*. "For now the *caudle*-cup is circling there."—Rogers' *Human Life*.

> Have you mark'd a partridge quake ?
> She cuddles low behind the brake.—*Prior*.

For the Yorkshire word cuddle the Lancashire people use "hutch," to signify pressing to the breast. "Come, *hutch* up closer to mi breast."—*Edwin Waugh.* It seems probable that a rabbit hutch is from this word, and means a closed-up place or chest, just as breast is also called the chest. And hatch has this same force, whether it be covering eggs, covering a deck, or covering a doorway.

(12.) AXE, to ask, from acsian (Anglo-Saxon). The modern "ask" is incorrectly formed by metathesis from "axe," as "task" is from "tax." In Old English both forms occur. (See Shakespeare's *Henry IV.*, part 1, act iv., scene 3.) In the Saxon version of the Gospels there is : "And ic acsige eow anre spræce." "What axen men to have?" says Chaucer, in his description of Arcite's death. The Earl of Southampton writes to Henry VIII., "I axed him." Margaret, the mother of this king, concludes a letter to him with "As herty blessings as y can axe of God." And Dr. John Clerk writes to Cardinal Wolsey : "The king axed after your Grace's welfare." "And he *axeing* a poyntel wroot seyinge, Jon is his name."—*Wyklyf, Luke* 1. Tom Hood jokes on this word; and the brothers Smith, in *Rejected Addresses*, have a similar play :—

> Jews from St. Mary Axe, for jobs so wary,
> That for old clothes they'd even axe St. Mary.

In Lancashire they use the word "spir," somewhat akin to "speer" (Scotch). King Alfred has in his translation of *Boethius* " He wile spyrian," where the meaning is, he will enquire.

(13.) REEK, for "smoke" *(rauch*, German ; *rec*, Anglo-Saxon), is connected with *rack*, to dissipate (exhalare), as seen in Shakespeare's " the *rack* dislimns," and in his *Tempest*, " leave not a *rack* behind." This rack is light, fleecy, and has nothing in common with "wrack" or "wreck," as many of his commentators assert, but comes nearer to the Scotch *rook*, "a mist." " The kiln began to *reek*."—Ballad of the *Felon Sow of Rokeby*. Shakespeare's " *reeky* painting" *(Much Ado about Nothing*, iii, 3) is explained as a painting discoloured by smoke ; and Edinburgh, from its smoky appearance, is facetiously termed " Auld Reekie."—See No. 97.

(14.) HAP means to wrap up, to make in a *heap*, to cover. "Which fast in hold hir *hapt*," wrote Gascoigne in his *Complaynt of Philomene*," where the meaning of the metaphor is, he kept her close in prison.

> I digged a grave and laid him in ;
> And *happ'd* him with the sod so green.
> —*Lament of the Border Widow.*

"His chaplain *hapt* him up in bed, and looked out of the window at the fight. There was no lull, neither was there any great advantage on either side. Only from the southward he could see fresh bodies of Danes coming across the plain."—Kingsley's *Hereward the Wake*, c. 24. Lap, in English, is to drink with the aid of the tongue, as all carnivorous animals do; for herbivorous animals sup by suction. But in Yorkshire, lap means to wrap, to cover up, like *hap*. The word is connected with lappel and lappet of a coat, the *folded* part. Milton explains it in the phrase "My mother's lap" (*Paradise Lost*); and it is in Latin "grembio natalis."

> As they sung would take the prisoned soul
> And *lap* it in elysium.—*Comus*, 535.

> And ever against eating cares,
> *Lap* me in soft Lydian airs.—*L'Allegro*, 136.

> The moon—with a cloud *lapp'd* all about her.
> —Hood's *Ode to Melancholy.*

I got a card and *lapt* it up handsome in a piece of taffata.—Selden's *Table Talk*, "Devils."

Writing, they serve to put under pies to *lap* spice in.—Burton's *Anatomy of Melancholy.*

The reason lap (Yorkshire) to drink, lappian (Anglo-Saxon) and lap (English) to fold or plait, lappe (Anglo-Saxon), are related, is because the tongue in lapping is folded. The Lancashire equivalent is *hill*, to cover; like the word *heal*, when we wish to say *recover* from sickness.

(15.) MUN for must, *maun* (Scotch) and the Scotch negative *maunna*, that carry out the analogy of "canna," "winna." There is a song in *Roister Doister* (A.D. 1566), in which the last line of every verse is "I mun be married on Sunday;" and the word occurs in *Minot* (temp. Edw.) : "Thai *mun* be met if thai war ma," which is almost Yorkshire. "For dole now I *mun* dye."—Ballad of *Sir Cauline.* " Ze *man* be war likeways with rhyming in terms " (King James I.)— *Essays of a Prentise.* " For work *maun* 'a gone to the getting whenivver money was got."—Tennyson's *Northern Farmer.* " Pass'd the first week an epoch will begin, a crisis which *maun* all thy care engage."—Dr. Maginn, in his *Father Prout's Reliques,* translated from "Vida's Silk-worm," 17.

There is a MUN used in the West Riding, which is exple-tive in such a phrase as, " Hy *mun*, tha's reight." In some parts it is pronounced *mon*, and has been explained as *man;* but this will hardly clear the difficulty when the address is to a woman, as it is at Leeds, as often as to a man. To me it seems to be *mun* for must, and is used as I have before said, as an expletive : a kind of positive acquiescence, as if one should say, " It must be so." A like difficulty is felt as to the origin of the Norfolk " bor," used in the same way and place by their neighbour-descendants, the Jutes. An East Anglian will say, " How be you, bor ?" whether addressing himself to a man, woman, or child. This Norfolk and Suffolk *bor* is, in Dutch, boer, and our English boor is distantly related. It is true, however, that the Anglian counties use *mor* sometimes to women and girls : which word is the Dutch *moer*, meaning lass or wench. About Leeds the affectionate address is *Ay lad*, or *Ay lass*, even if it is to an octogenarian. Some describe it as a contrac-tion of " neighbor ;" others of the familiar word " boy," like the negro of the United States, who is called by his master *boy* whatever his age. Truth is, the word is from the old Anglian *bohr*, " a pledge," and still survives in " borrow," " bargain," " neighbour." So that, like the Yorkshire *mun*, an expletive of strong assent, *bor* was simi-lar to the vulgarism, " I'll go bail what I say is true," or, " I'll be bound, I'm right." In the Heptarchy every man was bail or *bohr* for another ; hundreds, parishes, wapen-takes, lathes, ridings—in short, all county divisions were alike bail, pledge or bond, for the security of peace and the detection of crime : hence the word " neighbour," or bond for those near.—*Voisin* (French.) This bohr is seen in barter, bargain, borrow, neighbour, and *borowe*, an old word

for a pledge. Borough is of the same origin, as meaning
that members of such a locality are pledged to each other :
berga (Gothic), to secure. This must not be confounded
with the Icelandic *borr*, meaning a tree.

(16.) CAT-HAWS are the fruit and rough interior down of
the hawthorn, the cratægus oxycanthus, a common English
hedge plant. The cat is similar in meaning to the catkin
of the willow ; or, as hips and haws go together, the hip
being the *dog*rose, why, from a child's fancy, should not the
haws be a *cat*haws? The hip is the fruit of the dogrose,
or wild rose, rosa canina. The haw was heg or hag in
Saxon. As for the dog rose, I do not know when the dog
rose ! "The brembre flower that bereth the reede *heepe*."
—Chaucer's *Sir Thopas*, 1558, Wright's edition. The
Yorkshire couplet connects them with snow :—

> Hips and Haws,
> Frosts and Snaws.

(17.) WALSH (about Leeds) means the taste (or want of
taste) in bread without salt, and agrees with the Scripture
periphrasis "that hath lost its savour." A very expressive
word ; it has no equivalent in English ; for insipid, vapid,
mild, saltless, are by no means its equal in force. The
nearest word that represents it is in the Milanese dialect,
crôi, which signifies the taste of snow, if it has a taste at all.
Thus walsh would seem to mean a strange taste, as it is said
of bread made from dough with the salt omitted. In Scotch
it is "wersh as a potato without saut."—*Noctes Ambrosianæ*.
This walsh is a *dialectic* form of Welsh by the vowel change
(umlaut, in German) ; and welch formerly meant strange.
The Britons were Welsh (strangers) to the Saxons ; and the
Austrians even now call the Italians Wälsch and Italy
Wälschland. It is remarkable that wherever the various
Teutonic tribes intruded they denominated the natives as
strangers, a historical piece of impudence well authenti-
cated. The Abbé Sièyes says that the intruding Franks called
the natives Gauls or Welch ; and in a statute of an Anglo-
Saxon Guild, at Cambridge, in the 10th century, I found
" Gif hit thonne and do beran ealle gelice ; and gif ænig
gilda *hwilcne* man ofstlea," &c. This *hwilcne* Hicks latinises
by *wallus*.—See Hicksü thes. ling. sept t. ii, p. 20 ; see also

Thièrry's *Mérovingiens*, i, 143. In betting everyone has heard of a welcher, or stranger; as they say at Pudsey when a stranger passes: "Who's yon chap? A stranger. Then heave hauf a brick at 'em." "This castle of Leofric (the Saxon) was a building of a more solid and Norman type, such as had already been built for Edward the Confessor's French courtiers by the hands of 'welisce-men,' *i.e.*, French-speaking foreigners."—Kingsley's *Hereward the Wake*, c. i. He means Normans, and in King Alfred's will, the men of Dorset, Somerset, Wilts and Devon are styled Wealcynne, *i.e.*, Welshmen. Richard Waleys was Richard the Foreigner, the ancestor of our old hero William Wallace. Welsh (from a Sanskrit root) permeates through all the Aryan-descended languages and dialects; and as this stock-race migrated (or was driven) westward, it acquired the secondary meaning of westward. Accordingly the following places (and hundreds more) will be found (ancient and modern) in the west of their respective countries. Remembering Grimm's Laws of the commutability of letters —B for V, B for G, W for V—we have, amongst hundreds of words, *Wal*es (*Gall*es), Corn*wall*, Done*gal*, *Gal*way, *Wall*oon (in Belgium), *Bel*ge *Wall*achia, *Val*encia, *Gall*ia, *Gal*icia, *Bul*garia, *Wal*cheren, *Bel*ochecstan (the Wales of India), *Wl*och (Polish for Italy), *Wäl*shland (Austrian for Lombardy), *Wil*tshire, *Gl*oucester, Portu*gal*, *Bal*kans, *Gall*oway, Kirk*wall*, Ding*wall*, *Bil*boa, *Gall*egos, &c.

(18.) STEVIN, the voice from Stefnian (Anglo-Saxon) to call, an incretive of the verb Tefan, to cry.

> God that shope bothe erthe and heven
> I pray to thee that thou hear my stevin.

Towneley Mysteries, where it occurs again :—

> I heard by his stevin,
> He was sent down fro heven.

And Spenser :—

> And, had not Roffy renne to the steven,
> Lowder had been slaia thilkn same even.

(19.) STOOP, a post in the street, is from the verb stop, as stopping vehicles from passing on the causeway.

(20.) HEM is generally considered a vulgar contraction of them; but it is merely the Anglo-Saxon dative plural of *he*,

as *them* is of *the*. "Whiche they deservyd owther by con-
tricion and confession of her (their) offensis, or by the
remediis and helpinges of othir benefetis done for *hem*
(them)."—*Revelation to the Monk of Evesham*, 1196 A.D.
"And to *hem* give I faith."—*Chaucer*. "Much needeth all
shepheards *hem* to know."—*Spenser*. "And he (Zechariah)
gede out and myghte not speke to *hem*, and thei knewen
that he hadde seyn a visioun in the temple, and he bekenide
to *hem*."—*Wyklif's Bible*, Luke xiii. "Nay, better learn of
hem that learned be."—Spenser's *Shep. Kal. Nov.* "For
zee wyten welle, that thei that ben toward antartyk 'thei
ben streghte, feet azen feet of *hem*."—*Sir J. Mandeville*.
"Some put *hem* to ploughe, and some put *hem* to pryd."
—*Vision of Piers Ploughman*.

> And I had done a hellish thing,
> And it would work *hem* woe ;
> For all averred I had killed the bird
> That made the breeze to blow.
> —Coleridge's *Ancient Mariner*, 91-94.

A weird, supernatural, graphic imitation of the old ballad
style.

(21.) RIDING, the three divisions of Yorkshire, is from
trithing (Anglo-Saxon), a third part, as farthing is a fourth
part. Although this word has nothing to do with horse-
manship, it is often used as a joke in that sense :—

> If mine had been the luck in Yorkshire to be born,
> Or any of its *Ridings*, this would be a blessed morn ;
> But hapless one, I cannot *ride*—there's something in a horse
> That I could always honour, but I never could endorse.
> —Hood's *Desert-born*.

Here is fun and pun, but incorrect: besides, if born in
Yorkshire, it *must* have been in one of its Ridings.

(22.) ULLET (about Leeds) means a crying baby. "Ho'd
thi din, tha young ullet," says the mother to her yelling
child. It really means owlet, a young owl. The owl itself
gets its name because of its howl, which is strident: in
Latin, strix is a screech owl, and ulula an owl. It is clear
that all these words were invented to mimic the sound like
cuckoo from its cry. We have these derived words : to
yell, howl, to hail a person ; and to halloo (or hollow, as

the Cockneys pronounce it), and holler (as it is in Billings-
gate). We also get the invented word hullabaloo. At
Battersea College I remember a noisy student named
Hullah was asked if he were related to the famous musician,
John Hullah. A wag said "No ; he is related to hullabaloo." To shew the connection between owl and howl (and
yell) here is a joke :—A boy was yelling at the top of his
voice, " Oh would I were a bird," when that music-hall song
was in vogue. " So you was," said a Cockney, dropping
his h, as usual ; " So you was—a regular 'owl."

(23.) CROWDY (North Riding), called also stirabout and
porridge, is meal and water, or meal and milk, sweetened
with treacle or sugar. The word is formed from curd, by
metathesis, crud. It is referred to in the *Vision of Piers
Ploughman* (14th century) :—

> A few *croddes* and creyme, and a cake of otes,
> And bred for my barnes of benes and of peses.

The nobility and gentry of former days had bread of
wheaten flour ; the poor peasantry were content with bread
made of rye, oats, or barley ; and in most countries the
lower classes had an inferior mixture as the staff of life.
In Wales the lower orders had meslin, which was wheat
and rye ; and in Italy the Contadini have a favourite dish
called polenta, which is made either from maize or chest-
nuts, ground and eaten with roasted sparrows. This last
dish was also known to the Greeks, who called it alphiton ;
and the Portico, at Athens, where it was sold, was named
Alphiton Stoa : Aristophanes, in a comic way, designates
it Stoa Alphitopolis, *i.e.*, Porridge-town. The French make
their galette in a like manner ; and the definition of these,
Torrifacti hordei farina, answers to our crowdy.

(24.) KNAGGY (Yorkshire), cross when awoke from sleep ;
perhaps from gnawing, as in "knagging pain." In the
dialect of Barnyforth (County Wexford, Ireland), this word
is used with the same meaning, as seen in the following :—

> Fade teil thee zo lournagh, co Jone zo *knaggee*,

which may be translated, "What ails you so melancholy,
quoth John so cross." This Barnyforth, or Barony of
Forth and Bargie, was peopled by an Anglo settlement in

the reign of Henry II., under Strongbow, Earl of Clare.
The colony is still intact, unmixed and isolated; they speak
the language of that day (1170), never marry out of the
the barony, never suffer an Irishman to live with
them. Their language, or dialect, consequently is a fair
sample of the English of the 12th century. Colonel Ch.
Vallancey, the antiquary, is the only writer I know of who
has written of these people. His letter is dated 1783. In
the Milanese dialect this knaggy is gnec, evidently of kinship; and the Yorkshire nangnail, meaning where the nail
has been torn off deep into the flesh, is another form of
gnaw; the correct form is, however, agnail, from ange-nagle
(A. Saxon), pain and nail.

(25.) POTTER (in Dutch poteren, to stir) means to
fumble, to jumble from over-anxiety, hurry or senility.
Byron uses this word in the opening lines of his *Vision
of Judgment*.

(26.) "Lord deliver me fro' Hell, Hull and Halifax"
used to be a West Riding saw. As regards the first
place, not having been there, I can't say anything about it;
the second is the name of the river, and not the town—
Kingston-on-Hull; the third got its disreputable name
from its gibbet, which was at last swept away, with all its
horrors, by the uncrowned brewer of Huntingdon. Why
Hull is associated nominally with the other two, is perhaps
from alliterative sound, or there may have been at one time
an arcaneous reason for the triplet.

(27.) HAVERCAKE, an oatcake, from Havre (Danish)
oats. These havercakes are generally hung on a creel, a
kind of rack, and are termed haver-janok when dry. Near
Wakefield are lands which were formerly called Haver-
land. Coleridge, in his *Lay Sermon*, has "They are gone,
and with them the bristled *bear* and the pink *haver*." Bear
is barley, and haver, oats. Avoine (French), Avena (Latin
and Italian), Hafer (German), all mean oats.

(28.) GOB, a mouth, from *gabban* (Anglo-Saxon), to talk;
gab (Celtic), a beak; hence *gab* (Scotch), a mouth; *gobet* a
mouthful; *gober* (French), to swallow; like our *gobble*.
"Belching raw gobbets from his maw."—Addison's Poems.

The secondary meaning of talk gives us gabble, jabber, jaw, and jibe. Gaber and gabeler in the Romance dialect mean to gibe. The tertiary meaning of a simpleton is exemplified in gaby, gauby (Cumberland), like gauvin (Yorkshire), a person half-idiotic. Gauvison, in Yorkshire generally; gauvin, about Leeds; gaby, in London. In all Indo-European languages there are derivatives akin. English: gob, gab, gape, gobble, gobbet, goblet, guffaw (an open-mouthed laugh, loud and rude); French: gobe-mouche (one who metaphorically swallows flies, or, as the saying is, "Keep your mouth shut and you won't swallow flies"); "In bocca chiusa, non entran mosche" (Italian adage); German: gaffen, to gape, &c., &c.

Especially when he had taken too much to drink—which he did, after the Danish fashion, far oftener than the rest of Robert's men—he grew rude, boastful, quarrelsome. He would chant his own doughty deeds; and *gab* (as the Norman word was) in painful earnest, while they *gabbed* only in sport, and outvied each other in impossible fanfarronades, simply to laugh down a fashion which was held inconsistent with the modesty of a true knight. Bitter it was to her to hear him announce to the company, not for the first or second time, how he had slain the Cornish giant, whose height increased by a foot at least every time he was mentioned; and then to hear him answered by some smart, smooth-shaven youth, who, with as much mimicry of his manner as he dared to assume, boasted of having slain in Araby a giant with two heads, and taken out of his two mouths the two halves of the princess whom he was devouring, which being joined together afterwards by the prayers of a holy hermit, were delivered back safe and sound to her father the King of Antioch. And more bitter still was it to hear Hereward angrily dispute the story, unaware that he was being laughed at.—*Hereward the Wake.*

In Cumberland a noisy, open-mouthed fellow is termed a gob-slotch; and Mr. Sam Blackburn tells me that at Brighouse slotch is a drinking lout. To gape (another form of this Gob, *i.e.*, with the flat labial, sharpened) is in Flemish gaepen, to stare; because eyes and mouth open in partnership in the vacant expression of that kind of person: "Gaept niet rond ter wyl gy drinkt" (Flemish), "Stare not round while you are drinking." I have introduced this sentence from the Flemish because of the wonderful similarity between it and the Yorkshire dialect, especially of the North Riding. It was an old saying,

> Bread, butter, beer and cheese
> Are good English and good Frieze.

If you take into consideration the flat sibilant of the Somersetshire dialect, and the general vowel sound of the
Yorkshire, you have the old Flemish *(Walloon)*. Of course
the Friesland language is now superseded by the low
German, and near Groningen by Dutch, which is slightly
modified by a few idiomatic provincialisms. On a copper
box, in my possession, there are two engravings in the style
of the old German block prints, with this inscription in old
Dutch, " Iakop zent zyn Zoonnen na Egipte om koreen."
It is quite unnecessary to translate it, as the sound of the
words explains itself.

(29.) SHODDY, cloth made of the dust or fluff of woollen
goods: and this dust is called by a term more forcible than
elegant—" Devil's dust." *Shode* originally meant a tuft of
hair. " The nail ydriven in the *shode*" (Chaucer's *Knightes
Tale*) means the nail was driven through the hair into
the head, as Jael did to Sisera. The defrauding spirit of
those cloth dressers who use shoddy is mentioned even
so far back as Edward VI.'s reign: Bishop Latimer, in
his third sermon preached before the King (A.D. 1549),
makes particular mention of the thing and manner: "Thus
the pore gospel goeth to wracke. Yf his cloth be xviii yerdes
longe, he wyl set hym on a racke, and streach hym out wyth
ropes, and racke hym tyll the senewes shrinke a gayne,
whyles he hath brought him to xxvii yerdes. When they
have brought him to that perfection, they have a prety feate
to thycke him againe. He makes me a pouder for it, and
plays the pothicary, thei cal it *flouke pouder*, they do so
incorporate it to the cloth, that it is wonderful to consider,
truly a good invention": but this last ironicé.

(30.) CRAWDEN is a feat of daring, set by boys in play;
cradden in Lancashire, perhaps from *crad* (Welsh), vigour
or strength.

(31.) YONDERLY, about Huddersfield, means with a dis-
tant, vague and wandering look. This is an instance where
a dialect is more expressive than the mother-tongue.

(32.) SUER, for sure, is as old as the 12th century. It
occurs as an adverb in the *Revelation to the Monk of
Evesham* (circa 1196): "Trewly than he hylde me by the

right hand so *sewerly* as softly, and so clippid my hand in his."

(33.) STEE, a ladder (in Danish, *stige*), is from *stigan* (Anglo-Saxon), to ascend; and is seen in *stie:* "Ambition rash desire to stie" (soar).—*Faerie Queene*, ii, 3, 25. "Love can higher *stie* than reason's reach."—*Ibid*, iii, 2, 36. "Ne *steyrs* to *stey* one is none," *i.e.*, "There are no stairs by which to mount."—Chaucer's *Testament of Love.* "Or Christe went out of this erthe here, and *stighed* to heaven." —Gower. Connected with this *stee* are *stye*, a sore rising on the eyelid; *stye*, a raised hovel; *story* and *stair*, stirrup or stye-rope. "His leg bounde to the styrope."—*Wark-worth's Chronicles*, temp. Edw. IV. *Stile*, in a field, formerly written sti-gel; *stage*, a raised part. The Latin *stare*, to stand, with all its derivatives, are connected with the Teutonic root. About Wakefield they use *sty* for a narow road; a bridle-sty road is for horses only; *stya* (Anglo-Saxon), just the Norwegian *sti*, a path. In Danish, *sty* (as something raised) means clouds, and the verb̄ stige signifies to ascend. But in the same way that ignorant people make use of the redundant expression *ascend up*, so the Danes have *stige op:* however, though we cannot say, catachrestically, *ascend down*, in Danish there is a verb *stige ned*—perhaps because the verb has lost its primary meaning. "Stand down," says the counsel. The witness replied: "I can sit down or stand up, but I can't stand down."*

(34.) GET AGATE means to begin, to set to work. To go, is one of the most irregular verbs in the language, bor-rowing its past tense from another verb, wenden, to turn; in fact *to go* in all languages is most irregular (after *to be*). In Anglo-Saxon there were four verbs: gangan, wenden, yeden, faran; and these have got so mixed that comically you might say: I go, he went, we yede, they fare. Part of the German verb is ging. This gives us the old word ging, meaning a pack or flock. In the *Merry Wives of Windsor*, iv, 2, old Ford breaks forth: "There's a knot, a ging, a pack," &c., and Ben Jonson, in

---

* In stee, a ladder, the word *lad*der is connected with to *lead*.

his *New Inn*, i, 1, has: "I would not willingly see or be seen by any of this ging." The cognates in the Anglo-Saxon verb were: gangan, to go; gange, I go; eode, I went; gath, the imperative. From these we derive our words gangway, go, gone, pressgang. In old MSS. there occur frequently carucata bovata; these are translated oxgangs, or about a dozen acres each. In Lincolnshire there is "the Watergang Street, by the side of clear running streams," (see Kingsley's *Hereward the Wake*), and he has oxgang, holmgang, &c. "Either you are Hereward or you are his double-ganger" (c. 19), like the Scotch wraith or the Irish banshee (see No. 70). The numeral adverbs of order, as once, twice, thrice, four temps, &c., are in Norwegian and Danish, een gang, to gange, &c.; in German, einmal, zweimal, &c.; in French, une fois, deux fois, &c.; in Italian, una volta, due volte, &c.; in Spanish, una vez, dos veces, &c. Gate, a way through, formed like the Scotch ga'ed for gone. "A wee before the sun ga'ed doon."—*Lass of Gowrie.* "And hider gewat," *i.e.*, go-ed or went.—Bede's *Fragment of Cædmon.* "Ingate of the year" is Spenser's expression for the coming in of the new year. "Go your gait."—*Shakespeare.* In Scotch to "give a man his gate" is to let him have his own way; and the Yorkshire phrase "get out of my gate" is "get out of my way."

> O, dearest Marjory, stay at home,
> For dark's the gate you have to go.
> —Ballad of the *Spirit of the Glen.*

It will be seen that gate, now meaning the closed part of a way, was formerly the way itself: the latter meaning being formed by synecdoche from the earlier.

> And John is gone to Barnesdale,
> The *gates* he knoweth eche one.
> —*Robin Hood and Guy of Gisborne.*

Gates means *paths*. There is gait, which Puttenham (*Art of English Poesie*) defines "the manner of gate or going;" the Italians call it *andatura*.

> But they with gait direct to Lacon ran.
> —*Earl of Surrey.*

Shakespeare's "Stand not upon the order of going, but go at once," would be in Yorkshire "Get a gate agoing," and

in the Milanese dialect " *Metters adree a andaa.*"   In
Cædmon's Prayer there occurs " Er his eonon gange," which
may be rendered " Before his hence going."   " Go to their
gait, the Frenchman walks fast as if he had a sergeant at
his heeles."—Howell's *Instruction for Foreine Travaille*
(A.D. 1642).   Hood, with his usual felicity in puns, remarks

Keeper of gates that long have gone their gait.

"The criticks in *gates* and gestures will easily discover by
the comportment of a man's body whether he has learnt to
dance."—Basil Kennett's *Antiq. of Rome* (second ed. preface).   The grammatical present tense differs from the
colloquial.   We say "I am talking" as well as "I talk."
There are two tenses in English which are never mentioned
in books; but if grammar be a set of rules for correct
language, gathered from the best usage, then there ought to
be a proximate future and a recent past.   In colloquy
we express the former by the verb going, *aller*
(French), *sto per* (Italian), baan to (Yorkshire), and the
latter by *just; viens de* (French).   "I am going to
see your father" would be in French, *Je vais voir votre
père;* in Italian, *Sto per vedere il vostro padre;* in the
Yorkshire, "A'm baan ta see yer fayther;" and "I've
just spoken to my friend," would be in French, *Je viens de
parler avec mon ami.*   Before concluding with this verb go,
I may notice Agens, found in the old Mysteries, meant to
meet, to go towards; and from it we derive our preposition
against.   Again (an adverb) means literally to go once
more, like the auctioneer's going, going.   In the old words
Algate, though, and Nagate, in no manner, the affix gate
has the force of ways.   There are also Mabgate, Kirkgate,
Swinegate, Briggate, where gate means a way.   To gad is
to go about talking.   And Milton has "the gadding vine"
(Lycidas, 40 line), because of its wandering tendrils.   Long-
fellow in his *Golden Legend* has "the vagrant vine that
wanders," where he copies the blind poet, though the expression is redundant.   Wanton primarily meant wandering.
Milton speaks of Eve's curls as "wanton ringlets."

(35.) WEND, to go; from wenden (Anglo-Saxon).   It is
from this word we get the past tense, went, from the defective

verb, to go. Cockneys are sometimes heard saying "I ought to have went." This is old English, though not to be used now; as it would be wrong to pass old money, which, though good in its day, is not at present current coin of the realm. "To fetch water at a well is went."— Chaucer's *Clerkes Tale*.

> Thomalin why sit we so
> As weren overwent with wo.
> —Spenser's *Shepherd's Cal.*, March.

"The man having lately *went* out, had made it his business to trace it."—*The High German Doctor*, a whimsical, satirical book printed in 1719, and characterised by Pope in his *Dunciad* as scurrilous.

> How that the word is miswent.—*Sir John Gower*.

> But things miscounselled must needs miswent.
> —Spenser's *Mother Hubbard's Tale*.

Derivatives from this verb are wynd (Scotch), a passage; in Lancashire, wint; in old English, went; in Danish, gade is a street; ginnel (Yorkshire), an alley, from gone.

> But here my wearie teame, nigh over-spent,
> Shall breathe itself a-while after so long a went.
> —*Fairie Queen*, b. iv, c. 5. st. 46.

> This Troilus is by a privy went Into my chamber come.
> —Chaucer's *Troil. and Cress.*, iii, 786.

> Far under ground from tract of living went.
> —*Fairie Queen*, iv, 2, 47.

Near the peak of Derbyshire is a passage called Winnats, *i.e.*, the gates of the wind. Wind is also that which goes, hence the Evangelist speaks of the wind blowing, &c.: "Thou canst not tell whence it cometh nor whither it goeth." The window of a house was originally the aperture through which the wind blew, when glass was not; and to winnow was to separate chaff from grain by wind; to wind round and to wound round are actions like the eddying wind; to wander is to go. To wound is to make a missile go, and wound *(ferrito)* is the result of such going. Yeden (Anglo-Saxon) to go. "And I forth my way yede."— Wyatt's *Penetential Psalms*. "Far yaud" is the Scotch shepherd's cry to his dog to drive in the scattered sheep. "Before them yode a lusty tabrere."—Spenser's *Shep. Cal.*,

MAY. Wade, and its diminutive, waddle; *Guade* (Ital.), a ford by the common transmutation of G for W, are parts of this verb. In Arabic, Wady is a river, and the Spaniards got from their Moorish conquerors Guadiana, Guadal-quiver, &c.

FARAN (Anglo-Saxon), to go. "How fares it," like the German *wie geht's*, and the Flemish *Hoegaét het met u ;* farewell ; a thoroughfare, a way through ; ford (*i.e.*, fare-d), a shallow place through which you can go ; ferry fare, money paid for conveyance, and with cabmen the person so going ;* wayfare, events on your way ; fieldfare, a bird ; far, farther, further, forth, to further ; and all names of places ending in ford, as Chelmsford. In the Anglo-Saxon fragment of Bede, "For them ned-fere," is before his lower journey, meaning death.

(36.) To FRAME, means the same as "get agate," but with this difference, that the former indicates inaptitude and awkwardness.

> Oh dear ! A'm soa loath to begin,
> Yet t'wark mun be dun soin or late ;
> If A mean ta leave off I' good time
> A'm frame, an' am go get agate.— *Yorkshire Songs.*

"He could not *frame* to pronounce it."—*Judges* xii, 6.

> † To beg my bread from door to door,
> I wis it were a burning shame :
> To rob and steal it were a sin :
> To work my limbs I cannot *frame.*—*Heir of Linne.*

(37.) GUMPTION, meaning tact, knowledge, or what may be termed mental "knack," is from gaum (old Gothic), to understand ; and the opposite is gaumless, meaning silly or stupid. In the *Gospel of Ulphilas the Mœso-Gothic*, the passage in St. Mark xvi, 4, the word *saw* is "gaumidedum," with the signification of perception. In the Latin version it is "intuitæ," and in German "wurden gewahr." The expression "By gum" would thus seem to be "By my knowledge," as an asseveration not upon hearsay, but upon personal acquaintanceship. Common sense, or gumption,

---

* The Cockney Jehu said " I wants my fare !" and seized his fare by the coat collar : this was hardly *fair !* "Why, you've got yer fare, ain't yer ?" But cabby could not see the affair in that light.

tact. All other languages fail to give an equivalent to this
tight little expressive English phrase. *Nous* (Greek), *Chique*
(French), *Kuntnisz, Gemeinsinn* (German), *Accorgimento*
(Italian).

(38.) BAAN, in Lancashire beawn, and in English bound,
signifies prepared for an undertaking. The following
dialogue will show the meaning : "Where's ta baan?"
"A's baan daan taan to buy mi muther a peggy." Yorkshire is so large that one naturally expects to find a
difference in pronunciation for various localities. I remember a new boy from Pocklington came to a school at
Brighouse. One Saturday afternoon he was off to the town
without leave ; and this was the trialogue between him,
another, and the monitor :—

"Where's te baan ?"
"I's boun doun toun."
"Thah moan't talk i' that road, lad, na thah's cum here. Thah mun
say : 'A's baan daan taan.'"
Said the monitor : "You're both wrong ; say : 'I'm beoun deoun
teoun.'"

In the Old Chester Mystery play, the *Building of the Ark*,
Japhet says :—

> And I can maken well a pin,
> And with this hammer knock it in :
> Go we work bout din,
> And I am ready *boun*.

Meaning, "Let us set to work without noise, and I am
ready to begin." Most likely it is another form of bound,
boundary, bourne. A boundary of a parish is that sur-
rounding limit which you travel round, as in "beating the
bounds." Bourn, a boundary, is also a river—burn (Scotch)
—because rivers are amongst the natural limits of countries.
The Scotch ploughboy playfully translates his name Robert
Ruisseau. "That undiscovered country from whose bourne
no traveller returns," says Shakespeare, following *Catullus*,
iii, 11.

> Qui nunc it, per iter tenebricosum
> Illuc, unde negant redire quemquam.

In the old ballad of *Sir Cauline* the word is spelt bowne :
"Our King was bowne to dye." In Icelandic, *buinn* is to
set about a thing, the exact meaning of the Yorkshire baan.

(39.) MEASLES, the disease, Rubeola. Masel (German), a spot; the old English Mesel is a leper. In *Wiclif's Bible*, St. Matt. x, it is so translated, "Rase ye dede men, cleans ye mesels." Chaucer uses mesel for leper. About Halifax the people call the measles "Creas." "A bocher that selleth swyne's flesh that is anywise *mesell*, corrupt, or in the morayne, or if he by flesh of Jewes and sell it unto Christus men, and thereof the same bocher be convice, he shall greviously be amercyed," &c.—An old statute quoted by Stowe, vol. ii, p. 445.

(40.) BRIG for Bridge (brycg, A. Saxon). "Wherefor he loosede his gounes into the citee and brent at Algate and at Londone Brygge . . . and alle his hoste went overe at Kyngstone Brygge."— *Warkworth Chronicle* (temp. Edw. IV.) Briggate, at Leeds, is the street leading to the bridge over the river Aire. There are several Briggs in Lincolnshire, a Brigg near Ripley, and a Brighouse near Halifax. Will my Brighouse friends tell me where is the Brig? I know the locality of the *house*—it is in Prospect Place, or was !

(41.) PARKIN is cake made of oatmeal, carroway seeds and treacle, and is generally eaten at bonfire night, the 5th November.

> When Arthur, to make their hearts merry,
> Brought ale and parkin and perry.
> —Song of *Arthur o' Bradley* (1661).

(42.) SKELP, to strike, is a modification of slap; in German *schlap ;* which words have been formed by onoma-topy. "Some gat a skelp."— Ballad of the *Death of Featherstonhaugh* "To skelp and scaud poor dogs like me."—Burns' *Address to the De'il*. In the *Towneley Mysteries* Noah's wife says, "For dread of a *skelp* help will thi dam."

(43.) MOOTHALL was a common name for an assembly of people *met*, from *motjam* (Gothic), to discuss; hence to *moot ; moot* point, originally a question to be decided at the assembly ; *moot* hall, an old word found in Chaucer for the Council Chamber, and the present name of the Cloth Hall at Halifax ; folk*mote ;* burg*mote ;* witenage*mote*, the Saxon

Parliament or assembly of (wits or) wise men. From the
mixed class of people gathered at a meeting we derive the
word *mot*ley; and thence *mot*tled, meaning mixed, and
generally applied to a kind of soap. *Med*ley is another
form of the word.

> " Yonge men," seide Gamelyn, " this ye heeren alle,
> Sir Ote stant i' fettered in the moot halle."
> —Chaucer's *Cokes Tale of Gamelyn*, i, 807.

(44.) KNURR AND SPELL is a Yorkshire game, the origin
of which phrase is a hard nut for philologists to crack.
Could it be said to be connected with *Knorren und Spielen*
(German), the play of knob, the stick with which the knurr
is struck having a knob at the end? No doubt the gnarled
oak means knotty oak, and this gnar is another form of
knurr.

(45.) LAKE, to play, akin to *lac* (Saxon); *lek* (Scandinavian); *lacken* (old German), to leap; *lege* (Danish) to play,
has given us the English work sky*lark*ing. The *r* has been
erroneously introduced in *lark* (a spree), on the supposition
that it referred to the *alaudi arvensis*, or lavroc, and as this
bird mounts in the sky we have the second mistake, *sky*lark-
ing, for joking: but *sky*lark*ing* nowadays generally ends by
being *caged*, and those who indulge in such sport have to
attend to the *beak*.

(46.) HUMBUGS are those sweets which in London are
called brandy balls. Wallett, the Queen's Jester, in the
spring of his career, went round with these as refreshments
when acting in a barn. Addressing the solitary occupant of
the front seats (price 3d.), " Will you purchase any humbugs,
sir?" he received answer " Certainly not; humbugged
enough by the performance." This unkindness nearly
broke his heart, but, as he wittily observes, it was owing to
his neglect of Shakespeare's maxim, " Sweets to the sweet."
This humbug (not sweets), meaning to gammon a fellow, has
a curious connection with lake (to play) and barley. There
is a gammon meaning a side of bacon.

> But the knight gor'd him (*i.e.*, the dragon) with his spear,
> To make of him a tame one,
> And arrows thick, instead of cloves,
> He stuck in th' monster's gammòn.—Ballad of *St. George*.

This gammon of bacon is the Italian gamba, the leg; like viol di gamba, and the French jambon, ham. The gammon I refer to is connected with spinach (remember the ballad of *The frog that would a-wooing go*, with his rolly-polly gamon and spinach), just as barley, sesame, fernseed, fennel, &c. It is the Anglo-Saxon Gamen, a game as seen in backgammon, and in the ballad of *Sir Cauline*.

> And that thou never on Eldridge come
> To sport, gamòn or playe.—Ballad of *Sir Cauline*.

(47.) BARLEY, a Yorkshire word, to indicate a cessation of play for a time; a boy's truce. One writer thinks it is a coalition of the words, By your leave; another says it is Parley; and Sir Walter Scott explains it as a contraction of Byrlady, for by our lady (the Virgin Mary). There is a game in Scotland called Barley-brake, and Allan Ramsay writes, "While he cried "Barley-fummil," meaning, while he wished for a stoppage to the game. To me it seems clear that barley refers to the grain of that name, especially as fummil (or fennel) and sesame are also used in a mystic sense, the origin of which is lost. This sesame *(sesama* in Latin) is in reality an oil, expressed from the order of plants called Pedaliaceæ, and fennel is a kind of hay. Now it seems an odd coincidence that barley should be applied as a term for a cessation of play, fummil for the same purpose, and sesame as a figurative charm with which to open a difficulty: it is so used in the story of the *Forty Thieves*, in that classic of the Arabs, the *Thousand and One Nights*. If this explanation be unsatisfactory, I must plead that some of these dialectic expressions baffle the skill of the etymologist; and shall therefore say barley to this subject until more information be obtained. Feignalls is the London word for barley, and some think from the verb to feign, a cessation of play, but it appears to be fennel, a kind of hay. It is stated by Pliny that fern-seed had the power of rendering its possessor invisible; and Gerard, in his *Great Herbal*, published 1597, explains why it was believed to have this power. Ben Jonson has, "I had no medicine, sir. to go invisible, no fern-seed in my pocket *(New Inn*, i, 6); and Shakespeare, "We have the receipt of fern-seed, we walk

48 DIALECT OF THE

invisible."—*I. Henry IV.*, act ii, sc. 1. Æthelbert Binns gives a different meaning to Barley.

(48.) LOVER, about Heptonstall, means a chimney. The word primarily signifies an opening, as may be seen in the phrase louvre windows, which are openings in imitation of windows: the word has been formed on the epenthetic principle from *l'ouvert* (French), and was a window à l'ouvert, an open window. Another corruption is lubber boards, which are the boards running over such opening. It must not, however, be confounded with the seafaring phrase lubber; that is of Dutch origin, and was formerly spelt land-loper. "It' at the South ende of the same Hawle ys the Pryors Kechyn, which ys an olde Kechyn w[t] three *lovers* covered w[t] lede, and adjoyning to the same Kechyn ys there a Chamber called the South Sellerers Chamber."—*Survey of Bridlington*, by R. Pollard, temp. Henry VIII.

(49.) STARVE, to perish of hunger, in Yorkshire implies to be intensely cold. "A'm *starved* to deäth," like the Irish "kilt entirely," is nothing more than an expletive, and signifies being very cold. In the old writers it always means to die, like the Saxon *steorfan*, and the German *sterben*. "But Christ that *starved* for our redemption."— Chaucer's *Man of Lawes Tale*. "I pray to God that I might *starven* wood;" *i.e.*, die mad.—*Wife of Bathes Tale*. "The rather lambs be *starved* with cold;" "The early lambs are dead with cold."—*Shepherd's Calendar*, February.

> And on the border alle withoute
> Was writen on the stone aboute
> Leteres smale, that seiden thus,
> Here *starf* the fair Narcissus.
> —Chaucer's *Romaunt of the Rose*.

(50.) MAD, for vexed; and the diminutive verb maddle, to puzzle. "Shoo fairly seems maddled wheär all t' money goes."—*Yorkshire Songs*. Ariosto calls his epic *Orlando Furioso*, where furious, by a reverse process, stands for mad.

> Doan't be stunt, tak time,
> A knaw what maks thee so mad.
> —Tennyson's *Northern Farmer*.

(51.) To FEND, to provide for, from fandian (Anglo-

Saxon), to try. In the phrase "fending and proving" (no connection with defending), the meaning is, trying and proving; and to say a man is fending for his family signifies he is trying his best to maintain them. Forfend is, however, a hybrid word, Saxon and French. In Cumberland you may hear a man enquire "How fend ye?"

(52.) FRATCH, to quarrel, perhaps from fractus (Latin), broken; as we say, to break up friendship. Two batsmen at cricket had a tiff, and it was carried so far that a by-stander observed "they stopt i' t' middle o' t' wickets to hev a fratch." The word in Lincolnshire is lall, from laleo (Greek), to chatter; and flyte, in Lancashire, from flytan, to guard. A fractious child is a crying child. Whilst fractious is English, fratch is peculiarly Yorkshire. Differ, in Yorkshire, has the same meaning, and means the result of a fratch, like the word shindy. In Montevideo (a dialect Indio-Spanish) the word is *Barullo* (pronounced Barudjo); the good Madrilen says *Baraunda*.

(53.) DAD, for father (the diminutive being daddy), is from the Welsh *ei dad*, his father, declined thus: *ei dad*, his father; *ei thad*, her father; *vy nhad*, my father, where the declensions affect the initial of the word. "Come hutch up closer to me breast; aw'm thi dad."—Edwin Waugh's *Lancashire Song*. Derived words are generally direct from the genitive rather than from the nominative.

(54.) DELF, a stone quarry, from the verb to delve.

(55.) To PAWSE (near Leeds) and poise (near Halifax) means to kick. Whether this word be from peise, an old English word, to weigh down (hence avoirdupois), or pous, a foot; or pause, to rest; because the foot in the act of kicking is suspended in air, it is difficult to determine. When a boy I remember my schoolmaster explaining it as being from pause, to which I suggested that it might be from pous (the foot). The angry pedagogue threatened to illustrate the word, and added, in his striking manner, that he would make me "loup like a scopperel." Poyse occurs in Earle's *Microcosmographie* (A.D. 1628, articles 49 and 78), and means to weigh.

(56.) SCOPPEREL, a teetotum, is a diminutive of sceapan (Anglo-Saxon), to form or shape. The teetotum is a toy with numbers on its edges, and is twirled round by the fingers, and the numbers in total decide the winner in raffles or lotteries. This total or totum (Latin) was abbreviated into T, and thus by jingling assonance we get the word T totum or teetotum. In old English it was called a whirlbone or totum, and in French *un toton*. So, too, we get Ship or skiff, something distinct from a raft, otherwise how do we get the phrase ship-shape, except by assonance and affinity? Shop, something shaped, distinct from a stall; Landscape, a picture shaped with a view of land, tree, water, as far as the eye can reach. To scope out is to shape a hole. Scoup, Yorkshire for a skuttle, is from this word, of which Scopperel is a diminutive.

(57.) GAVELOCK, a crowbar. In the Cumberland ballad of *Jeff and Bob*, written by Anderson, there is "Nin leyke thee cud fling the *gavelick*." "Untille the Wallis (scil. Sir William Wallace) partie had umbelaid the brig, with *gavelockes* and dartes."—(*Peter Langtoft*, temp. Edw. II.) That witty specimen of the Lancashire dialect has a simile, "Stand as stiff as a *gablock*."—*Tim Bobbin*. *Gabel* (German) is a fork, and a coalrake is *ofengabel*. In Danish a fork is *gaffel*.

(58.) CRATCH, a wooden frame upon which pigs are killed; also a frame to hold eggs. Gantry is a wooden frame for beer barrels. Creel is a wooden frame for oatcakes and plates. Cratch-chair is one with rails at the back. About Brighouse, cratchy means very old. Cratch-cradle is a game of tying strings round the fingers.

(59.) NEIF, a fist; in Icelandic, *neifi*; *nœve*, in Danish; Scotch, *neef*. "Give me your *neif*" says Bully Bottom in *Midsummer Night's Dream*, iv, 1; and it occurs again in Shakespeare's *Henry IV.*, pt. II., ii, 4: "Sweet Knight, I kiss thy *neif*."

(60.) FETTLE.—"To be in fettle" is to be in the right trim, and "fettle to" means to set to work in earnest. "They fiercely *fettled* to the fight" occurs in the ballad of *John Elland of Elland*. The root of the word is *feat* or *fact*, meaning deed: for instance, Milton wrote "*facts* of arms;" Moore, "*deeds* of arms;" and Hood, "*feats* of arms." There are *facere, factus* (Latin and all its derived languages), but the want of such a verb in English is supplied by *do, make :* we, however, possess the participle substantive *feat*, of which *fettle* is a diminutive verb. This word occurs but once in Shakespeare, viz., in *Romeo and Juliet*, iii, 5. It puzzled the commentators so much that they proposed *settle* as the proper reading. The word occurs also in Hill's *Satires*, iv, 6,

> Nor list he now go whistling to the carre,
> But sells his team and *fettleth* to the war.

In the ballad of *Robin Hood and Guy of Gisborne* it occurs thrice :

> Then John bent up his long-behde-bowe,
> And *fettled* him to shoote.

> Yet neither Robin Hood nor Sir Guy
> Them *fettled* to flye away.

> When the sheriffe saw little John bend his bowe
> He *fettled* him to be gone.

(61.) SMITTLE and SMITTLING are confined to the West Riding, and signify to infect. *Smits* (in English *smut)* are falling flakes of soot ; and *smittle* is perhaps a diminutive verb formed from this *smit*, in Dutch *smouten*, to smoke as a chimney, and *smetten* (Dutch) to soil. In Norwegian *smuds* means dirt, and spot is *smitta* (Anglo-Saxon), and *schmutz* (German), while *smitta* (Gothic) and *smit* (Scotch) mean to infect ; *smitten*, to stain (Anglo-Saxon).

(62.) To STAUL is to bore, weary, tire out, satiate. There is no word in English that fully explains it ; and the nearest approach in any other tongue that I know of is *stuffà* (Milanese dialect) and *blaser* (French.) A Brighouse friend suggests that it is a metaphor drawn from a horse in the stall being overfed ; but I opine it is but another form of the word *stale*. This Milanese *stuffà*, the barbarous Latin *stuba*, came from the German *stube*, a room, a vapour-bath room, akin to *stue* (Norwegian), a room, hence it signified also to plunge, dive as in *attuffare* (Italian), and from the suffocating sensation experienced whilst under water *tuffa* meant to suffocate, and with the incretive *s*, *stuffa* is bored, stifled *blasé* (French).

(63.) Nomeny, formal words, a set speech, from *nomen* (Latin), a name. "Leave out that *nomeny*" means omit all that unnecessary verbiage. "Here th' justice said a *nomeny* to 'im."—*Tim Bobbin.*

(64.) Paddish, to coax. A friend informs me he heard it used under the following circumstances :—A horse had fallen heavily whilst drawing a waggon of stone; when it had risen the driver was about to lash it, but an old woman interposed, "Doan't flog it; you'd more like paddish it." I have heard it once at Rastrick, near Brighouse ; and never again.

(65.) Clam (Yorkshire and Lancashire word), to hunger, *klemmian* (Dutch), *klemt* (Danish), to pinch. Compare "terribly pinched," "at the last pinch," "pinching poverty." The real signification of Clam is to pinch, to stick together, hence *clammy*, in Dutch *klam* or *klamp*. Clammy lips are lips that stick together. Clam for hunger is the same, for the empty stomach pinches. In Anglo-Saxon, Clam was clay, because of its plastic properties. A klamp is an iron holdfast to hold two things together.

> Father clammed twice a week ;
> "God's will be done."
> —Eb. Elliott's *Corn Law Rhymes.*

> My entrails
> Were clammed with keeping a perpetual fast.—*Marston.*

> Now lyon's half-clammed entrails roar for food.—*P. Massinger.*

> Hard is the choice
> When valiant men must eat their arms or clem.
> —*Ben Jonson.*

> What, will he clem me and my followers ?--*Ben Jonson.*

About Leeds to pine, the same as clam about Halifax, means to hunger. "Ta see my awn bairns hauf pining fer brëad."— *Yorkshire Songs*, by J. H. Eccles. "The fiddler is just so many stringes above a beggar . . . . and his face is more *pyn'd* than the blind man's."—Earle's *Microcosmographie* (A.D. 1628).

(66.) Shive is a slice of bread; *schyve* (Dutch), *das scheibe* (German). Shakespeare, in his *Titus Andronicus*, has "Easy is it of a cut loaf to steal a shive :" no doubt he had in mind Proverbs ix, 17. *Shiver* really means to fall to pieces, and the second signification of trembling is paralleled by the phrase "to shake to pieces," and the nautical (? theatrical) term "*Shiver* my timbers." Walker explains *spill*, a shiver of timber, and Chaucer has *schivere*, a small slice : "And of your softe brede but a shivere."—*Sompnoure's Tale*, line 7422. The heckler speaks of shives of flax, made by breaking the fibres ; and Schiefer (German) among miners is a friable shale (not a shale that you can fry !) "He would pound thee into shivers with his fist, as a sailor breaks a biscuit."—*Shakespeare* (where ?). "Upon the breaking and *shivering* of a great state you may be sure to have wars."—*Bacon*. In Cockneyese this is *smithereens ;* and Carlo Porta in *On Miracol* has :

> Mi padron di tutt coss,
> Col meuv d'un me brasc
> Poss fav tutt in *spettasc*.

This Milan word, like all dialects, is very expressive— similar to the slang "eternal smash." The word shive is evidently another form of the verb to shave. Shag in Cumberland means a slice, and all smokers know that shag tobacco is the leaf sliced. While they speak about a shive of bread as a slice, they invariably say a "latherick o' bacon," about Holbeck and Hunslet ; and a "latherick o' fat," about Burmantofts and the Leylands, in Leeds.

(67.) Rue, to repent of, in English signifies pity, and the noun is ruth ; *reuen* (Teutonic).

> She whom I rewe my eyes did ever see.
> —*King James I. Phœnix.*

> When they to rewe their folie shalbe faine.
> —*King James I. Poems.*

Pretty Ophelia, in her mad fit distributing flowers to all, gives rue to the queen as a sign that she will repent marrying her husband's murderer. Greene, in his *Quip for an Upstart Courtier*, says "That rue which some might scorn in their youth, might wear in their age, for it was never too late to say miserere."

> But ever and aye my heart would rue,
> Giff harm should happen to thee.
> —Ballad of *Sir Cauline.*

> Rue on my child, that of thy gentleness,
> Ruest on every rueful in distress.
> —Chaucer.   *Man of Lawes Tale.*

(68.) ADDLE (Yorkshire), to earn wages, to *earn*, because
many got wages who have not earned them, from *edlean*
(Saxon), a reward. " The acceptable year," the day of yield-
ing again, is in Wiclif's version, " edleanes dœg." Old
Tusser gives a good use of the word :

> Where ivy embraceth the tree very sore,
> Kill ivy, else tree will addle no more.

Addle, applied to a rotten egg, is from *adlian* (Saxon), to
be weak and empty, and is connected with *idle*. The
Anglo-Saxon verb *adlian* is a repetionary verb, derived from
the Gothic *ata*, meaning to defile : *adl* (Anglo-Saxon)
meant pain.

> Parson's lass 'ant nowt, and she wëant a' nowt when 'e's dëad,
> Mun be a guvness, lad, or summat, and *a'dle* her brëad.
> —Tennyson's *Northern Farmer*.

(69.) Low, a blaze.

> The breth of hys mouth (*i.e.*, the dragon) that did out blow
> As yt had been a fyre on *low*.
> —Sir Degore, *written tempus Rich. I.*

This *low* is seen in whit*low*, which is a *white* swelling on the
fingers, and of a *burning* sensation. It is connected with
glow, as seen in glow-worm. In Scotland *alow* means *in
flames ;* *log* (Gothic), a flame ; *leoma* (Saxon), a flame ;
hence also *leman*, a lover, facetiously because the heart is
said to burn for love. *Lawen* (Teutonic), *hliwan* (A.
Saxon), mean to be warm, like the Scotch *lowe ;* from the
Teutonic comes the Icelandic *chloa*, with its gutteral aspi-
rate, from which are derived our *luke*warm, and all words
with the hard G initial that indicate warmth ; as glow, glaze
of an egg, gleam, glim, a Black Country word for a lantern ;
glory, glare, meaning both heat and an angry stare like the
Scotch glower ; gleed, a burning coal, &c.

> And forth upon his way he glood,
> As spark out of the bronde.
> —Chaucer's *Sir Thopas.*

Bearing in mind that the primary meaning is a little light,
we see how such words as gloom, loom, glimmer, glance,

glent (Scotch), glomb (Chaucer), and gloaming, the Scotch for twilight, are also derivable from the same word.

(70.) BOGGARD (Yorkshire word), for what is called in London Old Bogy, in Staffordshire Boget, and in French Croque-mitaine. As a child I well remember my French nurse sending me in terror to sleep whilst croning :

> Il faut être sage, sinon,
> Croque-mitaine, Croque-miton.

In Milan it is Giambell's Goat :

> Sont la cavra di Giambell
> Senza corna senza pell.
> Se la pell me mont in coo
> Salteroo feura e ti mangeroo.

In Spanish a bogy is Duende. The word is formed from bug, as dullard, wizard, sluggard, &c., are from dull, wise, slow, &c. That boggard is from bug can be seen at once in the equivalent bugbear ; bwg (Welsh), a goblin ; buka (Russian). To boggle at a thing means to do it in a hurry, as if frightened. This word bug, like grunt, sweat, and several other words, had formerly a poetical sound which is now lost. The "terror by night" (Ps. xci, 5), is in Matthew's version, "Thou shalt not neede to be afraid of bugs by night." Shakespeare frequently has the words, "What ho ! such bugs and goblins."—*Hamlet*, a. 2. "The mortal bugs o' the field."—*Cymb.*, a. 3. "Warwick was a bug that feared us all."—*Henry VI.*, third part, a. 2. The meaning is that Warwick was like a goblin that scared us. "Tush ! tush ! fear boys with bugs."—*Tam. Shrew*, i, 2 ; also in *Troil. and Cress.*, iv, 2. And Gosson, in his *Apologie for the Schole of Abuse* (1579), has this passage : "I am not so childishe to take every bushe for a monster, every shadowe for a bugge.

> Each trembling leaf and whistling wind they hear,
> As ghastly bug does greatly them afear.
> —*Fairie Queen*, ii, 3.

The writers of the seventeenth century generally used the word *mormo* (Greek) for bugbear. There is no doubt that bug (something terrible) in the course of time was applied to the domestic pest, as being itself a cause of physical terror. Milton in his *Comus*, line 617, has "monstrous forms ;" this in the first edition was "monstrous buggs": so says Beckford in his *Vathek*. The Americans apply the word bug to all beetles : and Poe's tale of the Gold Beetle appears in the United States as the Gold Bug.   Mr. Sam Blackburn, of Brighouse, writes : " Guytrash is an evil cow whose appearance was formerly believed in as a sign of death : it is also known as *padfoit*."   It is called *sworth* in Cumberland.—S. D.

(71.) SHO for she.

> Then Lucifer (*i.e.* the morning star) upsprang,
> Aurora's post, whom *sho* did send amang
> The jettie cludds for to foretell ane hour
> Before *sho* stay her tears.—Quoted by *King James I.*

"Some sadland a *sho*-ape."—*Scotch Ballad.*

> Rouewen so gent
> Be fore the king in hale *scho* went . . . .
> Be fore the king on kne sett
> And on hir langage *scho* him grett . . . .
> This Breg was the latimer (*i.e.*, the latiner or translator)
> What *scho* said, told Vortager.
> —*Peter Langtoft*, of Bridlington, Yorkshire.

The story is that Rowena spoke to Vortigern, and an interpreter explained what she said.

This *sho* sounds better than the Cockney dialogue :

Passer-by (to boys playing) : " What are you a-doing of ?   Ain't yer mother hollering for yer ?"
Chorus of Boys : " Her ain't a-callin' we : us don't belong to she !",

(72.) MISTER means business, and is sometimes spelt mistery, as in the " Trade and *mystery* of a goldsmith." " Canna beet (*i.e.* aid) a good fellow by your *mistery*," in the ballad of *Archie Ca'field*.   " Sebastian Cabota, esquier, governor of the *mysterie* and Companie of merchants."—R. Eden's *Translation of Munster's Cosmographia*, date 1553. " So he made the soldier's trade a *mystery*."—Selden's *Table Talk.*   " That which a man is bred up to he thinks no cheating : as your tradesman thinks not so of his profession, but calls it a *mystery*."—Selden's *Table Talk.*   " These are to certifie . . . by unskilfull persons that daielye sett upp trades and *misteries* in those things wherein they were never lawfull apprentices," &c.— *Warrant of Sir John*

Saville (temp. James I.) "And parents shall bring up their children in the *mysteries* of their own trade."—Burton's *Anat. of Mel.* And in a schedule for income-tax, which I am at this moment filling up to my sorrow, I find "art, mystery, adventure, or concern," collocated. These, as remains of old words, are still retained on the statute book for varieties of business. When Duguesclin fell into the power of the Black Prince, his friend Carvalay offered to pay his ransom. This Duguesclin refused, saying : " *Quil ne comptait point avec bon compagnie ; mais si j'ai mestier, je vous prierai.*" This *mestier* meant want. But even the English business has two meanings, occupation and want. What do you want here ? is the same as what business have you here ?

As to *mister*, it occurs in

> Of knights and lefdyes honest,
> Of burges and of jonglors,
> And of men of such mesters.
> —Adam Davy's *Alexandre* (temp. Edw II.).

"What mister men be ye ?"—*Chaucer ;* here it signifies sort. "What ever myster man am I ?"—*Romaunt of the Rose.* "And other things that misters were."—Barbour's *Bruce IV. ;* here it means wants, and corresponds to the Spanish *menester.* Of this word mystery there are three forms (trimorphic), of different origin ; but from their meanings having mutually reacted upon each other they have become identical in spelling. 1. Mystery, meaning occult, from *mysteria* (Greek), *mystère* (French). 2. Mystery, the old Miracle plays, in which the "ministri ecclesiæ" took part. *Mistère* (French). 3. Mystery, a business *ministerium* (Latin), *métier* (French), *mestiere* (Italian). As a trade is called a craft, as craft has acquired the meaning of cunning, and as cunning is a kind of privacy, the popular idea has intermingled all three words with a sense of secrecy. Hence Hood puns thus : "No mister (business) in the world and yet no mistery." In Yorkshire, "what mister ?" means what kind.

(73.) BASS, a kind of mat, generally called a rug in London, is akin to the Belgic *bies*, which is a rush ; hence our word *besom.* In German, *besenreis* is the mat-weed with

E

which the *besen* (besom) is made ; and the last part of the word *(reis)* is our *rush*, or, as the Scotch write, *rash*.

> Green grow the rashes, O."—*Burns.*

In Spain the dustman *(basurero)* calls every morning for your dust *(basura)*.

(74.) SPERRINS are the banns asked in church. " Hes ta put in t'sperrins?" means, have you been asked in church. It is part of the old verb to *speer, i.e.*, to ask questions. The original meaning of the word speer is a hole in a window or shutter, through which a person might peer or look, and that served the purpose also of letting in a little light. So that speer is an increative of peer, to peep, the initial *s* having this power in hundreds of English words. To speer, as a hole in the shutter, occurs in the moral ballad of the *Heir of Linne :*—

> And when he came to Ihon o' Scales,
> Upp at the speer then looked hee ;
> There sate three lordes upon a rowe,
> Were drynking of the wyne soe free.

In the *Acts of English Votaries* it means to shut, because the hole in a door or a shutter is useless to see through unless the door or shutter be shut : " The dore thereof oft tymes opened and speered agayne." The changes in meaning are reasonable, and as might be expected, from well-known laws that govern the alteration in the signification of words. Thus : 1. Speer, a hole in the shutter, to look through ; 2. looking through ; 3. as looking is for the purpose of obtaining information, the word began to mean inquire. It is now obsolete, except in the Yorkshire derivative sperring : the banns.

(75.) SEG is said of potbellied rabbits suffering from tubercular peritonitis. In London a workman uses the word sag, meaning bending by its own weight.

(76.) BRAY is to hammer (see Proverbs xxvii, 22); and though never heard out of Yorkshire, it is a word well understood by all English people. Some peculiarities connected with this word deserve notice. Bread is corn brayed out into flour ; broad is the result of braying a thing out flat, and applied in the abstract it means extension.

What is brayed is broken (bray, break, breach). In Saxon, *brecan* is to break.

(77.) BATHROLL, sweets, so-called from being round in shape, and resembling a bathbrick in colour. The London name is colt's-foot rock.

(78.) TOOGY (about Leeds), *wee* and *weist* (about Hull), and *canny* (about Thirsk), are like tiny, or very little indeed. The equivalents are: In French, *tantin ;* in the Milanese dialect, *ciccin ;* in Cumberland, *lall ;* Danish, *lille ;* Spanish, *pequeño.*

> He hath but a little wee face.—*Shakespeare.*

Canny in Scotland has more the force of careful. I once saw a sugar basin with the motto, more homely than polite, "Be canny wi' the sugar." Near Stokesley a man once speaking to me of Little Heaton and Roseberry Topping, described them thus: "*Canny* Yatton's t'heighest hill in a' Yorkshire ; an' o' th' top o' Roseberry it's as cau'd as yeis i't yattest day i' summer." *Wee*, connected with *wenig* (German), little, occurs, too, in Heywood's *Fair Maid of the West ;* and in the *Wisdom of Dr. Doddypole* (1600 A.D.), it is "Some two miles and a *wee* bit, sir," which the Scotch would term a bittock.

(79.) SWELTED means intense perspiration, from *swelan* (Anglo-Saxon), to burn. Hence swelter, a poetical word, and its derivative, sultry. The Yorkshire word sweal for the guttering of a candle when exposed to a draught.

> Nor has our hymeneal torch
> Yet lighted up his last most grateful sacrifice,
> But dashed with rain from eyes, and *swaled* with sighs
> Burns dim.—*Congreve.*

> Sweltered with everlasting dog-days.—*Bentley.*

Is the sun to be blamed that the traveller's cloak swelts him with heat ?—*Bishop Hall.*

> Parch'd and sweltering in the westering wind.
> —Milton's *Lycidas.*

> Rude Acheron, a loathsome lake to tell,
> That boyles and bubs up swelth as black as hell.
> —*Sackville's Induction*, st. 69.

There is a verb *sweltan* (Anglo-Saxon), to die ; and its derivatives are not to be confounded with those from *swelan*, to

burn. The following quotation contain these : " Woe that
made his heart swelt."—*Chaucer*. " Crist that swelt on the
rood for the sake of man's syn " *(Minot)*; meaning, Christ
that died on the cross for man's sin. " Swiltit thi ana."—
Cœdmon (A.D. 680), as quoted by Boniface in one of his
letters ; and the passage may be translated, " Died he,
therefore, lonely."

(80.) EE and EEN mean eye and eyes: the Yorkshire
plural is formed regularly, according to the Anglo-Saxon
nouns of the simple order. " Fore him schul wepe mone
an *e*," by John Audley, the blind poet: written at the
Monastery of Haghmond, A.D. 1426. " Alas, I see not one
unvail his *ene*."—*King James I.* " And daulphins, seahorse,
selchs with oxin *ee*."—*King James's Sonnets VIII.*

> Come, thou monarch of the vine,
> Plumpy Bacchus with pink eyne.
> —Shakespeare's *Ant. and Cleop.*, ii, 7.

" Tommy, hes tha seen a chap wi' one *ee*, called Green ?"
enquired Billy ; the answer was, " Noa, Aa hannot: what
wor t'other *ee* called ?"

(81.) COBLIN, a round lump of coal ; in Lancashire a
cob, and about Brighouse *nub*, while at Rastrick a great
nubby is a great novice, both connected with knob. Round
paving stones at Leeds are termed cobble-stones. The
root of the word is *co* (Welsh), a round lump ; and *cobian*
(Welsh) is to beat, hence cudgel. In the Cornish mines
the girls who break the tin ore are called cobbers. Mr.
Gaskell gives a ludicrous account of a trial for assault at
Manchester. One witness says : " If um had cobbed um
as um did um, um'd oather a kilt um or um um." The
phrase, " that beats all," is, in Lancashire, " that cobs a';"
and cease pelting is " give o'er cobbin." The game of
cob-nut is derived from this Welsh *co*.

(82.) " THE REGISTER OFFICE," a farce in two acts, by
Joseph Reed. In this he gives the broken English of a
Scotchman, an Irishman, a Frenchman, and a Yorkshire
girl, in the Cleveland dialect.*

---

* See *Glossary of Cleveland*, by the Rev. J. C. Atkinson, Incumbent
of Danby-in-Cleveland,

ACT I.—Mr. Gulloch sits in his office.

Enter MARGERY.

Mar. Sur, an' I may be so bold, I'se come to ax an ye've sped about t'woman servant, 'at ye advertised for?

Gul. I have not. Come nearer, young woman.

Mar. Let me steek't deer, first, an ye please. *(Shuts the door.)*

Gul. What countrywoman are you?

Mar. I'se Yorkshire, by my truly! I was bred and bworn at Little Yatton, aside Roseberry Topping (Little Heaton, in the North Riding).

Gul. Roseberry Topping! Where is that, my pretty maid?

Mar. Certainly God! ye knaw Roseberry? I thought ony fule had knawn Roseberry. It's t'biggest hill in oll Yorkshire; it's aboun a mile an a hofe high, and as coad as ice at top on't i' hettest summer's day; that it is.

Gul. You've been in some service, I suppose?

Mar. Ay, I'll uphole ye have I, ever sin I was neen year ald. Nay, makins, I'd a God's penny at Stowstah (Stokesley) market, aboun hofe a year afore 'at I was neen; and as good a servant I've been, thof I say't myself, as ever came within pair o'deers. I can milk, kurn, fother, bake, brew, sheer, winder, card, spin, knit, sew, and do every-thing 'at belangs to a husbandman, as weel as onny lass 'at ever ware clog-sheen; and as to my karecter, I defy onybody, gentle or simple, to say black's my nail.

Gul. Have you been in any place in London?

Mar. Ay, an' ye please; I lived wi' Madam Shrillpipe, in St. Pole's Kirk-garth, but was forced to leave my place afore 'at I had been a week o' days i't.

Gul. How so?

Mar. Marry, because she ommost flighted and scauded me out o' my wits. She was t' arrantest scaud 'at ever I met wi' in my bworn days. She had seerly sike a tongue, as never was in ony woman's head but her awn. It wad ring, ring, like a larum frae mworn to neeght. Then she wad put hersel into sike flusters that her face wad be as black as t' reeking-crook. Nay, for that matter, I was but rightly sarra'd, for I was telled aforehand, by some verra sponsible fwoke, as she was a mere donnot; howsomever, as I fand my money grow less and less every day (for I had brought my good seven-and-twenty shilling to neen groats and twopence), I thought it wad be better to take up wi' a bad place than no place at all.

Gul. And how do you like London?

Mar. Marry, sir, I like nowther egg nor shell on't. They're sike a set of fwoke as I never saw with my eyn. They laugh and flier at a body like onything. I went no but t' other day ti t' baker's shop for a lafe of bread, and they fell a giggling at me, as I'd been yan o' t' greatest gawvisons i' t' warld.

Gul. Pray, what is a gawvison?

Mar. Why, you're a gawvison for not knowing what it is; I thought ye Londoners ha' known everything; a gawvison's a ninny-hammer. Now, do you think, sir, 'at I look ought like a gawvison?

Gul. Not in the least, my pretty damsel.

Mar. They may bwoast as the will o' their manners, but they have nea mare manners than a miller's horse, I can tell them that ; that I can. I wish I had been still at canny Yatton.

Gul. As you have so great a liking to the place, why would you leave it ?

Mar. Marry, sur, I was forced, as van may say, to leave t'. The 'squire wad not let me be. By my truly, sir, he was efer after me, mworn, noon, and neeght. If I wad but ha consented to his wicked ways I might ha' had gould by gopins, that I might. "Lo' ye, 'squire," say I, "you're mista'en o' me ; I'se none o' thea sort o' cattle ; I'se a vartuous young woman, I'll assure ye ; ye're other fwokes fwoke ; wad ye be sike a taystrel as to ruin me ?" But oll wadn't do ; he kept following and following, and teasing and teasing me. At length, run I telled my auld dame, and she advised me to gang to London to be out of his way ; that she did, like an onnist woman as she was. I went to my cousin Ishell, and says I to her, "Ishell," says I, "come, will thou goway to London ?" and telled her the hale affair atween me and the 'squire. "Odsbeed !" says she, "my lass, I'll gang wi' thee ti t' warld's end." And away we come in good yearnest.

Gul. It was a very virtuous resolution. Pray, how old are you ?

Mar. I'se nineteen come Collop-Monday.

Gul. Would you undertake a housekeeper's place?

Mar. I's flaid I cannot manage't, unless it were in a husbandman's house.

Gul. It is a very substantial farmer's in Buckinghamshire. I am sure you will do ; I'll set you down for it. Your name ?

Mar. Margery Moorpout, an ye please.

Gul. How do you spell it?

Mar. Nay, makins, I knaw naught o' speldering. I'se nea schollard.

Gul. Weil, I shall write to him this evening. What wages do you ask ?

Mar. Nay, marry, for that matter, I wadn't be ower stiff about wage.

Gul. Then I can venture to assure you of it. You must give me half-a-crown, my pretty maid. Our fee is only a shilling for a common place, but for a housekeeper's we have always half-a-crown.

Mar. There's twea shilling, an' yan, tea, three, four, fave, six penn'orth o' bross, with a thousand thanks. God's prayer light o' you ! for I'se seer ye'rt best friend I have met wi' sin I come frae canny Yatton, that you are. When shall I coll again, sir ?

Gul. About the middle of the next week.

Mar. Sir, an' ye please, gud mworning to you.   [*Exit.*

(83.) GARTH, a yard or surrounded place, either by wall, fence or houses, &c. Margery here calls St. Paul's Church-yard "St. Pole's Kirk-garth ;" and I remember when a boy having a "feight in Smithies' brick-garth," in Leeds. Cognate words are garth, girth, yard, garden, gird; all from the Anglo-Saxon *Gyrdan*, to surround (cingere. Latin). Garth is Norse, and yard is Anglo-Saxon.

(84.) WHERRY is a large four-wheeled cart without sides, and is termed a lorry in the Midland counties. Vans are used in London as wherries are in Yorkshire. As a boat, it is a different orthographic form of ferry; in Latin, *horia*. Ex. gr.

> And in his oaken cup doth float as safe as in a *wherry*.
> —Drayton's *Nimphidia*.

(85.) CLUTHER, to gather in a heap; in Lancashire clutter, from *cluder* (Welsh) a heap, and *cluderiaw* to heap together. Hence also clot (of blood), and clouted (cream).

(86.) LIG (to lie down) has a weight of authority in its favour, and once possessed a dignity which admitted it in poetry.

> But ah, Mecænas is yclad in clay;
> And great Augustus long ago is dead,
> And all the worthies liggen wrapt in lead.
> —Spenser's *Shepherd's Calendar*, October.

> And said his beasts should eat enow,
> And ligg in grass up to the chin.
> —*Ploughman's Prologue*.

> Liggen in his hood.
> —Chaucer's *Sir Thopaz*, 15,319 line.

> The joyous time now nigheth fast
> That shalt allegge this bitter blast.
> —*Shepherd's Calendar*, March.

> Settys me downe and grankys and gronys
> And lyges and restys my wery bonys.
> —*Towneley Mysteries*.

> Methuncheth that Deth has done us wronge
> That he so soon shall ligge still.
> —*Elegy on Edward I*. (MS., date 1307.)

> An he made the bed has he ligs on, afore he comed to the shire.
> —Alfred Tennyson's *Northern Farmer*.

It is the fashion for philologists, where they are in doubt as to the origin of a word, to rummage the dead languages, and when they find a root somewhat similar it is emphatically stated that the word in question is evidently a derivative of the latter, forgetting that the Scandinavian is as old as the

Latin or Greek, or the earlier Etruscan and Palasgian, and it is just as probable that the latter have borrowed from the former as that the Aryan has been indebted to these. There are certain words common to humanity, as mother, father, sister, brother, &c., which have percolated through all tongues of all ages from the first language spoken to the present day. These words may have become changed, modified, or transformed, according to the peculiarity of nations by which certain organs are more in use than others; but still a sufficient resemblance is to be seen. Take for instance the following word, which is panomphic:—*Night* (English), *nyx*, *nyktos* (Greek), *nox, noctis* (Latin), *nht* (Hebrew), *neet* (Yorkshire), *uoche* (Spanish), *nocc* (Milan), *nôs* (Welsh), *nocht* (Irish), *nicht* (Scotch), *noch* (Russian), *niht, nyht, næht, neaht* (Anglo-Saxon), *notte* (Italian), *nuit* (French), *nat* (Danish), *nacht* (German and Dutch), *nosch* (Sclavonic), &c.*

Returning to the word lig or lay: its original has given to the Greek *logos*, a word, to the Roman *lex*, or *legis*, a law, for the genitive is really the primal part from which languages borrow, if they borrow at all. That law should be connected with lie or lay is clear from the extant phrase, "to lay down the law." It has given to the later Roman (the Italian) *lege*, and to the modern Frenchman *loi*, and *ley* Spanish, and to the English law, low, lie, lay, alloy, lee, lees, leg, and to lag, which is putting down the leg in a dilatory manner. What is a log but a tree laid down? Rely is to put trust in, to lie on another for support. It also gives us the Yorkshire word lug (the ear), for that member in man *lies* down, as distinguished from those of beasts, which are erect.

(87.) LUG, the ear. In Scott's "Fortunes of Nigel," the eaves-dropping hole that King James had built to listen to the prisoners' talk is called the *lug*, and a similar one of Dionysius is termed by the same king "Dionysius' lug."— *Ch.* xxxiii. As the British Solomon is discoursing of this

---

* In an opposite way, *to cut* differs in all languages. Try we a few: English *to cut*, Italian *tagliare*, French *couper*, German *schneider*, Greek *tome*, Latin *cædere*, Spanish *cortar*, Anglo-Saxon *sciran*, Welsh *llwch (?)*, Russian *padstreegy*—very expressive and mellifluent this last word—eh?

lug, he suddenly turns to a bishop present and asks : "A lug—d'ye ken what that is, my Lord Bishop?" The Lord Bishop (ruling passion, of course), answers : "A cathedral, I presume to guess," which so startled His Majesty out of all propriety that he bursts forth, "What the deil, mon," &c.

> Ye high, exhalted, virtuous dames,
> Tied up in godly laces,
> Before ye gie poor Frailty names,
> Suppose a change o' cases ;
> A dear-loved lad, convenience snug,
> A treacherous inclination—
> But let me whisper i' your *lug*
> Ye're aiblins' nae temptation.
>
> —*R. Burns.*

Lug is another form of *lig*, to lie down. The ears of man are laid flat, and cannot be raised at will, like those of beasts. This lug (a noun) gives to lug (a verb); in Suevo-Gothic, lugga is to draw, to pull. To lug means to pull the ears: "An' by the *ears* most terribly him *lugs*."—*Drayton's Moon Calfe.* About Leeds it always means to pull by the hair, like the Italian *accapigliare* ; but in English it implies to pull forcibly by anything, hair, ear, coat or cuff. In the West of England *sowle* means to pull, drag or lug. In Shakspeare's *Coriolanus*, act iv., 5, occurs the expression : "Sowle, the porter of Rome, gates by th' ears" It is conjectured the word originated in the phrase taking a *sow* by the wrong ear. "Venus will sowle me by the ears for this." —*Love's Mistress*, A.D. 1636. "A lieutenant *soled* him well by the ears (this is the Yorkshire lug), and drew him by the hair about the room," and this is the Italian accapigliare.— *Strafford Letters*, vol. ii, p. 149. It must be borne in mind that Anglo-Saxon words were not borrowed from the Latin or the Greek ; rather the other way ; for the Latin is a mere modern language when compared with the remote antiquity of the Anglo-Saxon, or at least its original, the Gothic. The Scandinavian had a language and a home long before Romulus and Remus were suckled by the wolf.

(88.) STUNT (Northern Counties) obstinate.

> Don't be stunt, tak time.
> A knaws what maks the sa mad.
> --Tennyson's *Northern Farmer.*

(89.) LURDANE (old English), *lourdin* and *lourdant* (old French), means stupid, clownish. "Lurdans or clowns attired in their workyday clothes."—*Floris. translation of Montaigne*.

> In one, red after-revel, droned her lurdan knights slumbering.
> —Tennyson's *Idylls :* "Pelleas."

(90.) SKINNY, avariciously mean, perhaps because a mean man is said to be a skinflint, which last word is explained as one who is so miserly that he would skin a flint, if possible, although he should spoil a knife in so doing.

(91.) BRANDY SNAP, very thin gingerbread, sweet and brittle, which is sold at fairs in the Northern counties. It is something like what Londoners term jumbles, but is in large cakes two or three feet long. Brandy snap is as great a treat with the French, who call it *pain d'épice* when soft, and *du croquet* when brittle. The German *schnapps* is, however, a dram.

(92). SNOD, smooth and even, has the same meaning in Scotland ; and a snood is a fillet with which a young girl binds up her hair, smooth and neat. Had Dickens any such notion of evenness of character in his thoughts when he named one of his immortal Pickwickians, Mr. Snodgrass, *even* in temper and *green* in experience?

(93.) RAILY, about Leeds ; fairly, about Halifax, as expletives, mean very much indeed ; corresponding to the Milanese propé, from the Latin propè.

(94.) STAKE, to shut, is from *steken* (Dutch), *stecken* (German), and in Lancashire *tin*, from *tynan* (A. Saxon). Hence town, an enclosed place, as towns formerly were, and Chester now is. Tun is a barrel to enclose liquid, and to tunner is to barrel up.

> And after that made Argus for to tyne all his windows.
> —King James I. *Phœnix.*

(95.) TO FELL is to knock down, vellen (Dutch), fällen (German), and connected with fall. "For fell folk did shoo well," from the ballad of the *Felon Sow of Rokeby*. From this verb is derived the word field, being properly land where the trees have been felled. There is this difference between fell and fall, like set and sit, lay and lie, raise and rise, drive and drift, and the two cognate verbs to hang, that the first verbs of these pairs are active transitive, and the latter are neuter intransitive.

(96. RANT is senseless vociferation, and has given us the sect called Ranters. The original meaning of rant is to sing, from ran (Icelandic), a song, and it still keeps this meaning in Scotch: Rune (old Norse). Burns is facetiously called Rob the Ranter, by Allan Ramsay, and Tennant, in his *Anster Fair.*

(97.) RAUGHT is the hee-haw of a donkey, and is from *reach*, to stretch, the neck being extended when "raughting." In the same way, to *reach*, or eructate, tendency to vomit, is to stretch the neck (see Boken, No. 4.) *Raught* from *reach* is analogous to caught from catch. In Barbour's *Bruce*, bk. viii, it occurs for snoring: " But fell in sleep and routed high." In Icelandic Raute is to roar like a wild beast. About Wakefield there is another form of this word, viz., *rack*, which is applied to the Broad *Rack* of the Calder: on the Thames a stretch or expanse of water is called a *Reach;* and the Wakefield form of the word is seen in the Danish *Skaggerrack.* About Halifax *reach* becomes *raik*, as in English we have match—make, batch—bake, &c. This word *rack* is seen in the phrase *on the rack*, the rack being an engine of torture on which the limbs were dislocated by stretching. The distaff for stretching out the wool was called the rock. Shakespeare's magic "cloud-cap't towers" has "leave not a rack behind," *i.e.*, a light, fleecy, stretched-out cloud. This so puzzled the commentators that they thought of substituting *wreck*, especially as the Avonian Bard had been speaking of the fading of solemn temples, gorgeous palace, great globe. Addison also speaks of the "wreck of worlds" But wreck and rack have no affinity. The origin of *rack* is racan (A. Saxon), to reach: in Dutch it is *rek* (see No. 13). That raught and reach are the same can be seen from many instances. Cooper in his wonderful book, *The Purgatory of Suicides*, iv, 20, has

> My spirit, freed
> From matter, seemed an enterprise to speed
> Once more, across Death's gloomful ocean wave ;
> And *raught* the shore !

Spenser, speaking of a robe reaching to her heels, has:

> It raught down to her lowest heel.
> —*Fairie Queen*, v. 5, 2.

And Chaucer says:

> Her tresses yellow, and long straughten,
> Unto her heels down they raughten.
> —*Rom. Rose*, v. 1021.

Here *raught* means reached, straught means stretched. Straight means stretched (see *Euclid*, bk. i, def. 4). Raught was in old English pronounced *raft*, and we have the word *rafter*, beams that *reach* across the roof, and *roof* is that which stretches over a house. Chaucer rhymes *draught* and *raught* in his *Prioresses Tale*.

(98.) THREAP, a quarrel, is *thrap* (Lancashire), *theapian* (Saxon), perhaps on the ground that "Two are company but three are none." It occurs in the old ballad, "Take thine old cloak about thee," which is quoted by Iago, in *Othello*:

> It's not for a man with a woman to *threape*.

Surrey and Chaucer have *threpe*, and it means to shout. The American *Argufy* and the Milanese *Tacca lit* are the exact equivalents. "Some cry upon God, some other *threpe* that he hathe forgoten theym."—*Bp. Fisher*. "Dinmont still lingered, twisting his hat in his hand; 'It's no for that, sir—but I would like ill to be bragg'd wi' him—he threaps he'll bring a score o' witnesses and mair.'"—*Guy Mannering*, ch. xxxvi. In Scotland "an auld threap" is a superstition obstinately persisted in of old: like the Corsican vendetta. Burns speaks of Tam o' Shanter's wife "nursing her wrath to keep it warm." In Spanish it is reñir; and it corresponds to the London expression "to have a grievance."

(99.) TOKEN OR PLEDGE. These words imply a bond, or something *taken*, in Dutch *Teeken*, for a fulfilment of a promise made. The commercial world, we are told, is kept rotating by the power of credit; it seems that man's confidence in man is not so boundless, for we have a long list of words of this kind. We have *bail* in a police-court, *bounty* for soldiers and sailors, *mortgage* for property, *hypothec* in Scotland, *surety* and *sponsor* for children at the font, the

Queen's shilling for enlistment, *pledge* for pawnbrokers, *token* for permissive money or earnest money, *godspenny*, *arless (a Yorkshire word for a pledge)*, *pawn*, *bondsman*, *bound*, hence the phrase " I'll be bound for it," *wages* (or gages), for service (we wage war), *banns* for marriage, and *borowe*, an old word that meant a pledge or bond. " And I will be your borowe."— *Vis. of P. Plowman.* " I pray God and Saynt Nycholas that was my borowe."—*Dives and the Pauper*, ii, 9. " Baile nor Borowe."—*Shepherd's Calendar*, May. "For though ye borowes take of me."— Chaucer's *Romaunt of the Rose.* The godspenny is money given to servants at the Statute Fairs, as an earnest of engagement, and is in German *Dienstpfennig* (service money), or *Aufgeld.* " I drawe ye to record, lords, he said : with that he cast him a godspennie."—Ballad of the *Heir of Linne.* In French this would be *denier-à-Dieu.* There is a custom in Carlisle : a godspenny, or piece of silver, is presented to the Dean and Chapter when an exchange of the tenant under a lease is required. Pledge is in French *arrhes*, derived from *arabon* (Hebrew), *arrhabo* (Latin), *arrabon* (Greek); these correspond to the German *Pfand*, Dutch *Onaerpandt*, and *Vorantwortung*, and seem to be something like stipulation when a straw *(stipula)* was given as a pledge. In Italian *arra* and *pegno.*— *Vide* Gen. xxxviii, 17 ; II. Cor., i, 22 ; Ephes. i, 14. As before stated, *Pfand* (German) is a bond ; now pinfold is *Pfandstall*, or placed in bond till the animal be redeemed or bought out. So we say a person in prison is in bonds. As a remembrancer of bond for the transfer of land there was an old custom that several boys should be present as witnesses, and each boy had his ears well pulled ; this custom still exists in Berkshire. A similar practice is when the overseers of a parish beat the bounds ; they are accompanied by many of the children, who receive a cuff to remind them, and as " a pledge to assure them thereof." The Germans have *daraufgeld*, and the Italians *la caparra* for a deposit on hiring a coach. Wedding, a religious compact or pledge (now civil); wed (A. Saxon), wad (Scotch). Wed (A. Saxon) was a pledge, hence the phrase " And therefore I plight thee my troth ;" bet, a contract to pay a sum on a venture ; wager, an agreement; *wadset* (Scotch), *a mortgage;* these are closely connected, and vary in form depending on the national channel through which they have flowed—thus : The Scandinavian *Wed* becomes *Vadiare* (Latin), Wædian (Anglo-Saxon), *Guadiare (Romance dialect)*, *Gaggier (Provençal)*, *Gageure* (French), wage and gage (English). These are *in recto ;* and *in obliquo*, *Wed* (Scandinavian) becomes *Bad (Damnonian dialect)*, *Vet* (Danish), *Wette* (Belgic), Bet (English). These derivations are not forced, but from the known transmutation of the W into G (wage, gage), and V into W or B *(wahr* and *versus*, govern and *guberno)*. They have been formed according to the peculiar laws *(Grimm's Laws)* depending upon the predominant use of one set of the oral organs more than of others, according to various nations. We know for instance a Frenchman speaking English will most likely pronounce death, det ; a negro's massa becomes boss ; a German will change father to fader ; and a Chinaman has metamorphosed business into pigeon. Pinfold and to Pen.—In the Grays Inn Road, London, is a public-house called " The Pindar of Wakefield," which word puzzles Cockneys, who are better acquainted with Red Lions and King's Heads. Pindar is the man who impounds stray cattle He was also a character in *Robin Hood and Maid Marian :*

> The father of Robin a forester was,
> And he shot in a lusty long bow
> Two north country miles and an inch at a shot,
> As the Pindar of Wakefield does know.
> —Ballad of *Pedigree of Robin Hood*.

Here the ballad-monger is exact to an inch, but is he not drawing the long bow with his two miles ? Sometimes it is spelt Pinner, as in the ballad of the *Baffled Knight :*

> O, yonder stands my steed so free,
> Among the cocks of hay, sir ;
> And if the Pinner should chance to see,
> He'll take my steed away, sir.
>
> Upon my finger I have a ring,
> It's made of finest gold—a ;
> And lady, it thy steed shall bring,
> Out of the Pinner's fold—a.

In Rabelais I find *Opignérer*, to impawn or pledge ; and a

gentleman from Limoges once gave me a Limousin saying :
" Nous dimittons nos codices et vestes opignérées," meaning,
we will put our books and clothes in pledge.

(100.) MIDDEN is a dunghill : Mödding (Danish), a
dung-heap.

> A snug thack-house, before the door a green,
> Hens on the midden, ducks in dubs are seen.
> —Allan Ramsay's *Gentle Shepherd.*

" Ower middens and ower dykes."—*Christ's Kirk on the
Green,* attributed to King James I. (A.D. 1437). " No
more than the sonne that schyneth on a myxen."—Chaucer's
Lands. Ms. There is an old proverb " Better wed over the
mixen than over the moor," which is in Scotch " Better wed
o'er midden than o'er moss." Here we have both forms of
the word. The Germans have a similar proverb : "Heirathe
über den Mist, so weist der wer sie ist." A modern poet
writes " And cast it on the mixen that it die."—*Idylls of the
King ;* Enid. Mexen, in Lancashire, means to clean a
stable. This mixen is connected with *mix* and the Latin
mingere, and would seem " quis est miscela omnium ali-
mentorum." The root of the word has produced the
following : in English, among, mingle, mongrel, mix, minx
(una cattiva donna che fa la piscia, ed altre cose sottintese),
muck. But it must not be supposed that these words are
derived from mingere (Latin), but rather from the Anglo-
Saxon, which had three cognate verbs for *mix :* Micsan,
to mix dung ; micgan, to mix muck ; mengan, to mix
anything.

Hereward laughed bitterly. " I suppose one will murder the other
next, in order to make himself the stronger by being the sole rival to
the tanner. The *midden* cock sole rival to the eagle ! Boy Waltheof
will set up his claim next, I presume, as Siward's son ; and then
Gospatric, as Ethelred Evil-Counsel's great-grandson : and so forth,
and so forth, till they all eat each other up, and the tanner's grandson
eats the last."—*Hereward,* c. xvii.

The Danes term the oyster-heaps left by the Aborigines
(prior to the Scandinavians), kjokkenmöddings. The
Saxons and the Romans borrowed from the primary :
Mæso-Gothic. As a last quotation, which will show that
mix and mixen are akin, I take a passage from Paynel's
Regiment of Helth. " The operation of the stomake is to

make a good myxyon of things there in, and to digeste
them well,"—of course, like compost.

(101.) SAIM is lard or hog's dripping; in Welsh it is *seim*.
In the East Riding you may hear of a "blether o' saim,"
that is, a bladder of lard. A joke is: A woman in Hull
sold butter, and it was *saim* in the middle. What a shame,
you will say: but it was *same* in the middle, of course.

(102.) BRADES O' ME means like me; perhaps it is
formed from "such a breed as me."

(103.) BRIM, applied to the wind, means bleak, keen.

> Eft when ye count you freed from fear
> Comes the breme winter with chamfred brows.
> —Spenser's *Shep. Cal.*, Feb.

And in a Saxon MS. (Harl. Coll.), quoted by Warton, who
dates the ballad 1200, it occurs:—

> With lokks lefiche and long,
> With front and face feir to fonde
> With murthes monie mote her monge,
> That brid so breme in boure.

Thomson, imitating the older poets, writes, " The same to
him glad summer or the winter's breme."—*Castle of
Indol.*, ii, 7.

(104.) GROIN, a pig's snout. In the *Towneley Mysteries*
there occurs "two swyne gronys," and to groin in old
writers means to grunt; so that *groin* was transferred from
the *noise* to the *nose*. The old word *grunt* was applied to
human beings as well as to swine, and had a sense appli-
cable to heroic poetry. Hamlet speaks of man as
grunting and sweating. No doubt this gives us the modern
groan.

(105.) HALCH, a noose, is from *hals* (Danish), a neck,
the noose being thrown round the neck.

(106.) HIDE, to beat, where giving one a hiding is like
the slang phrase to tan one's hide. The metaphor is
paralleled in the phrase to leather a person—the hide being
undressed leather. Besides, we speak, too, of giving a boy
a dressing.

(107.) SWILLINS, pig's wash, connected with the verb to swill—to drink immoderately.

(108.) TENT, to prevent, like the old English *let*, to hinder.

> I stacher'd whyles, but yet took tent ay
> To free the ditches.—Burns' *Dr. Hornbook.*

(109.) THICK, friendly; I suppose metaphorically taken, for friends stick close together.

(110.) To PAN, meaning in old English to join together; to set to work, to get accustomed to a thing. As, "Tha'll hev to pan to t'job;" again, "That 'll du when it's getten pann'd to thy head." Perhaps a dialectic form of *pain*, meaning you will have to give yourself the pain to do it *(Donnez-vous la peine*—French), or take pains.

(111.) NAP, a sleep, or forty winks, from *hnappian* (Anglo-Saxon), to slumber. This word, which now has a facetious meaning, was once grave and heroic. Wiclif's *Bible*, Psalm cxxi., 4, speaking of slumber, has "Lo, he schall not nappe, neither slepe that kepeth Israel." In the Dutch version it is "En sal niet slupmeren noch slapen," where the two verbs come nearer to the modern version of slumber and sleep. Nappy was a drink that induced sleep. "And drink good ale, so nappy."—*Wyatt* (1503 to 1542). "Thenne wythe a jugge of nappye His knyghts dydd onne hymm waite."—Chatterton's Ballad of *Sir Bawdin.* "But I have nappy beer."—Crabbe's *Parish Register.* "While we sit bousing at the nappy."—*Burns.*

> Care mad to see a man sae happy,
> E'en drown'd himself amang the nappy.
> —*Tam o' Shanter.*

> She breweth nappy ale.—Skelton's *Elinor.*

In Yorkshire they use the word *nap* as a threat, in the way we say "You'll catch it;" this is from *nab*, to take, as seen in "Hob and nob;" this phrase meant originally "Have it or not have it," but is now a convivial expression. For instance, one of the laws of Ina (see Wilkins *Concil*, p. 59. *Leges Inœ*. *De pugnis*), begins:—"Gif hwa gefeohte on Cunninges Huse, sy he scyldig ealles his yrfes, and sy on

F

Cynninges Dome, hwæther he lifé *age* the *nage.*" That is,
"If who fights in King's House, be he fined in all his
possessions in the King's Court, whether he lordship *have*
or have not." This is the older form of hob and nob.
Besides, Shakespeare writes "Hobnob is his word; give't or
tak't." About Leeds to naup is to hit on the head; and
the boys of that town have an irreverent cognomen for a
church verger, viz. : dog-nauper ; like the Spanish church
beadle, *perrero* (perro meaning a dog). The old talkative
bishop of King Edward VI.'s time has "Straight ways he
was taken and *naped* in ye head."—Latimer's *Sermons.*

(112.) YORKSHIRE-BITE is the name given by Londoners
in general, as a dubious compliment to our natural sharpness. This is not to be taken as an isolated case, for most
towns, counties and countries, have peculiar names, sometimes self-dubbed, otherwhiles contumeliously applied by
others. Liverpool gentleman, Manchester man, Bolton
chap and Wigan fellow are dignified, manly, familiar and
depreciative, as we descend the scale. Something akin to
this were the Belgian characteristics described in Monkish
Latin verses :—

> Nobilibus Bruxella viris, Antverpia nummis,
> Gandavum laqueis, formosis Burga puellis,
> Lovanium doctis, gaudet Mecklinia stultis.

In my own native town we were generally denominated
Leeds-loiners. As a boy I used to be told that this referred
to Marsh Lane. The system is old : the Athenians were
nicknamed gapers; those quidnuncs were always "goup-
ing" for information.—Vide *Acts of the Apostles,* xvii, 21.
So to Christian Rome the people of the villages
(pagus) were Pagans, because Christianity reached the
country last : this word during the Crusades was corrupted
into paynim. And the same cause in England named the
people of the heaths, heathens. The Spanish Creole of
Mexico sneers at the Spaniard of old Spain under the name
Gachupino, just as those we designate Yankees retort on
us with Britisher. Voltaire says the Spaniards called the
French Gavachos, who retaliated by calling the Spaniards
Maranas. One from Buenos Ayres is a Porteño, and one
from Montevideo is Oriental, which latter is the name

arrogated by John Chinaman. John Bull calls his cousin across the water Jonathan. Our Australian Queenslander is a Cane Crusher, a Sidney-born is a Corn Stalker, and a Tasmanian a Gum Sucker. More in my book on Nicknames, shortly to be published. Who has not heard of the Cockneys of London, the Muscadins of Paris, the Biricchini of Milan, or the Gauchos of the Argentine?

(113.) WICK is from the Anglo-Saxon *cwick*, life or motion. It is remarkable that as motion represented life, so stillness or quiescence figured death. Quickset hedge, quicken, still-born, quicksand, sable mouvant (French), arena movediza (Spanish), quicksilver, to touch to the quick, be quick is also to look alive, vite (French) meaning quick, is akin to vital; and vivement (French) is both lively and quickly; quicklime, cal viva (Spanish) as opposite to slaked lime, and quagmire from quake to move. A funny story is told of a village in Yorkshire where the people, seeing a hedgehog for the first time, sent for "Canny Lee," a poor lame man, who was said to know " a dollop." When brought to the place in a wheelbarrow, he examined it on one side ; and some one present opined that " it's a soart o' moinstane." " Hod thi din, mun," replied Canny Lee, " till a've seen it reight. Wheel me to t' other sade." On being wheeled round, he shouted, " It stirs. A'm sewer it's *wick*. Wheel me hoam agaen." This Canny Lee was also called Coddy Queer ; and this reminds me of a saying of his : "As queer as Dick's hatband ;" and if you expressed surprise, it was added "because it went nine times round and wouldn't tie." Of course not, somebody would have to tie it, as it could not tie itself. See? For the word wick see also No. 132. In the ballad of the *Yorkshire Horse Dealer* I find—

> " T'oud codger 'll niver smoak trick.
> I'll swop wi' him my poor deead horse for his *wick*."

Hood in his *Death's Rambles* has etymological fun and witty pun on quick (living) and quick (swift) :

> Death met a coachman driving his coach
> So slow that his fare grew sick ;
> But he let him stray on his tedious way,
> For Death only wars on the *quick*.

The quick and the dead.—*Apostle's Creed*.

Men and beasts and fowls with breath are quickened.
—*Dryden*.

One of the fires queinte and quickened again.—*Chaucer*.

Wick (as Hackney Wick) is another word altogether, from *vicus* (Latin), a village or a street. In Anglo-Saxon wic means a dwelling.

(114.) ARRAND, a spider, about Halifax, is like (Rabelais) *araine* and *arraignée* in modern French, though the whimsical monk also writes *asterion*, after Pliny. In Lancashire it is *eddicop* or *eddicrop*, which seems like the *attercoppa* of the Anglo-Saxon, and the *eddercop* of the Danish. The meaning would appear to be poison-head—*ætter* (Saxon) poison. Among the Lancashire people a person with a bad temper is said to have an attern-temper. Compare this with our phrase, "To poison one's mind." This *cop* connected with *caput*, head (Latin), is found in cap, cope, chapter, capital, capper (Cumberland), one who excels, which was shad in Anglo-Saxon, capt (Yorkshire), puzzled, like the Latin *mentem capere*, and the Italian *mentecatto ;* and to cop (Norfolk). "I could have copt 'm at their pates."—*Bloomfield*.

(115.) To WARE is to spend money, from the noun *ware* as seen in its compounds warehouse, earthernware, &c. Ware was the Anglo-Saxon word for goods.

(116.) HIPPIN, in London a napkin, is properly that which covers a baby's hips.

(117). ALLYBLASTER, for alabastor, which derived its name from a town of that name in Egypt, where this mineral was first obtained. This Yorkshire word is so written in a list of articles at Bridlington Priory by Rych Pollard, 32, Henry VIII., " *Small tables of alleblaster and imag's.*" Boys shorten the word into alley, as they do tawny into taw. A saying I used to hear, when a child, was—

> Snaw, snaw cum faster,
> White as alyblaster ;
> Poer owd women, picking geese,
> Sending feathers daan ta Leeds.

Stony and marble explain themselves.

(118.) THRONG means very busy; *dringhen* (Dutch), *throng* (Saxon), a crowd. Who so busy as people in a crowd?

> Besides, that place of motions is so *throng*,
> That one will scarce have end a thousand yeare.
> —*Nature's Embassie, 1621, Braithwaite.*

(119.) ASKERD is a lizard. Dry askerd is a land lizard, called a swift in Essex, from the rapidity of its motion; and water askerd is the newt or eft.

(120.) ROARING and BELDERING signify crying in a loud way, and had once an heroic sound which is now lost.

> Sit thee down and roar:
> For thou hast killed the sweetest innocence
> That e'er did lift up eye.—*Othello.*

That these words had their origin in onomatopy is clear: compare them with the synonymous Cumberland phrase "Roaring and belling." Bêler (French) is to bleat; bellow is the noise of the bull; and bull, bell, bawl and beagle (an old word for a young bull) all indicate either a noise or something that causes a noise. In the same way *cry* means both to shout and weep.

(121.) BEESTING, from *byst* (Anglo-Saxon), is the first milk of a cow after calving.

> So may the first of all our fells be thine,
> And both the *beesting* of our goats and kine,
> —*Ben Jonson's Hymn to Pan.*

> And now, besides, her *beestings* never fail
> To store the dairy with a brimming pail.—*Dryden.*

(122.) To MOOR, means as a cow does when her urine is mixed with blood. The medical name is *hæmaturia*.

(123). DRAPE is a cow not with calf, or one which gives no milk, and is to be fatted.

(124.) CLUMP, a mass or clod. All the Norse families of languages have this word in common—*klumbr* (Icelandic), *klump* (Swedish), *klomp* (Dutch), *klompen* (Flemish), *der klump* (German). Yorkshire folks speak of "clumping up land down;" and a Lancashire man makes use of "a clump of wood." Clogs are generally called clumping clogs. Stowe remarks, "He brought his wooden shoes or clampers with him." The technical word in joinery, clamp, is from this root; so is clumps, a numskull. The following dialogue, from *Tim Bobbin*, will show the meaning of clump :—

SHE : Well, when yo getten there, yo'll may happen see eawr Thomas ; and yo'll tell him we'n had the shantry mended and a new pigstoye belt, un at we dun pratty weel beawt him.

HE : Belie' me, Meary, dost think at aw's nowt for t'do bo go clumpin up an doeawn t'skoies a seechin' yore Thomas ?

Henshall praises Collier, of Rochdale (the author of *Tim Bobbin)*, and calls his work one of great original humour, besides being of great advantage to the student of Saxon literature. However, his fanciful derivations from the Belgic, Welsh, and Saxon are not to be implicitly followed.

(125.) NOONINGSCOPE is a luncheon, perhaps nuncheon or a slight refection at noon, the same as luncheon is a repast at eleven o'clock ; *el once* (Spanish).

(126.) GET SHUT ON is to be rid of.

> An' he ain't got shut on him yet.
> —Tennyson's *Northern Farmer*.

(127.) FASHION in such a phrase as "How could you fashion to beg?" Fash in Scotland is to bother. "I canna be fashed" is "I can't be bothered." "My affaires and fasherie would not permit me."—King James I., Preface to *Exercises at Vacant Houres* (A.D. 1591)

(128.) COCKLETY means easy to upset. There is no English equivalent for it. Rickety, the nearest in meaning, implies a weakness in the parts, whereas a thing that is cocklety may be quite strong. Tottery means weak in the legs. There used to be a street rhyme, I once heard it in Mabgate, Leeds :—

> My owd grandmother, she is dead,
> She teach'd me to mak cocklety bread.

Totter (physically) is dodder (mentally), and in Yorkshire becomes *dother*. Can anyone explain this cocklety bread ?

DITHER.—" T' whole place fair *dithered* agean wi t' clapping an' shouting when Aa stood up ta speik." "Bud when he oppened t' parcel he *dithered* it across t' room."—*Pogmoor Almanack*. I used to hear the word *gender* in my young days. "When t' wind blaws it maks the winders

gender again." Dodder or *dother*, as also *dander*, a nasal-
ised form of *dadir*, together with our word, are connected
with Old Norse *datta*, to vibrate, palpitate, as the heart
does ; Swedish *datta*, *dutta ;* and these, probably with *dua*,
to be in a state of motion.

> I dase and I dedir,
> For ferd of that taylle.—*Towneley Mysteries.*

Compare Dutch *sitteren*, German *zittern*, and Old Norse
titra : to tremble from fear or cold.—[A. Binns sends me the
foregoing.] In English we tremble from fear, shiver from
cold, and our teeth chatter from either cold or fear. This
dodder has a diminutive, *dottrel* (not *dotterel*, the plover).

> Wherefore good Reader, that I save them may
> I now with them the very Dottril play.
> —Bunyan's *Divine Emblems*, 9th ed., 1724.

(129.) Posy is a flower, or a bunch of flowers. It was
formerly the motto or love-verse in the *Language of Flowers*
sent with the nosegay ; in that meaning it was another form
of the word poesy, *i.e.*, the motto.

> What posies for our wedding rings,
> What gloves we'll give, and ribbonings.
> —Herrick's *Hesperides.*

" We make a difference between suffering thistles to grow
among us, and wearing them for posies."—*Dean Swift.*

(130.) Slack, not having much to do, is a nautical
metaphor, from the fact that when a rope is left slack it is
not fulfilling its purpose. It also means not very busy, not
having much to do. Slack coil is small coal and dust.—
Fanny Dyer's favorite joke.

(131.) Sucker is sugar and treacle boiled together, and
differs from toffy and butterscotch. The London hardbake
is something similar, but contains split almonds. The word
is evidently from *sucre* (French), *zucchero* (Italian), *azucar*
(Spanish), *saccharum* (Latin). Bellman-sucker is generally
said to be a good beating with a strap, administered to the
urchin sent on an April-fool errand, something like "pigeon-
milk."

(132.) Powse means worthless, from *pws* (Welsh), the
refuse. In Lancashire there are powsedirt and powsement.

This word becomes paus in Hunslet. By the way, it is a curious coincidence that in typography pause and clause seem to be connected in sound with paws and claws of beast and bird. George Blackburn pointed out to me the remarkable resemblance in the French mèche, a wick, and méchant wicked; though there is no derivational affinity (see also No. 113).

(133.) BAKIN SPITTLE is a wooden shovel with which to turn the bread when baking. This spittle is a corrupted form of *spatula*, a flat knife, which last word is a diminutive of *spartha* (Latin), a flat broadsword. The Greek *sphathe*, the Latin derivatives, the Italian *spada*, a sword, and the English spade, are all from some Teutonic word— which?

(134.) DOLLOP means a large quantity, and is from deal, in Anglo-Saxon *dœlan*, to divide, to deal out, as we still say in card playing. Deal is now restricted to mean *much* and *many*, whereas it formerly meant any quantity. Accordingly, in old authors, we meet with such phrases as "a small deal," "half deal," "some deal," "more deal." In this the Yorkshire *dollop* is consistent, being a modification of the word to give an extended signification.

(135.) SWATHE is the outside husk, and even the rind of bacon. The swathe, some say, ought to be sward.* In Anglo-Saxon there were *sweard*, a turf, sod, and *swathe*, a bandage. The Leeds-loiners use swathe.

> The heavenly Babe you there shall find,
> To human view displayed ;
> All meanly wrapt in *swathing* bands,
> And in a manger laid.—*Xmas Hymn.*

St. Luke, ii, 7, has "swaddling clothes," and so has Keble's *Christian Year.* Th and D are commutable letters, and in many Saxon words with the "D barré," as the historian Thierry calls it, present English has simply the D. Accordingly we have *swaddy* for the contemptuous name of a soldier, from the clothes in which he is swaddled or dressed. "When carpet *swads* devour ye soldiers spoile." — *Whetstone*, A.D. 1557.

---

* See Æthelbert Binns' Yorkshire Dialect Words, in the *Leeds Mercury*.

(136.) KITTLE, by metathesis, is tickle.

> It never fails, on drinking deep,
> To *kittle* up our notion
> By night or day.—*R. Burns.*

As a verb, it also means to bring forth kitten or " kitlins,"
as Yorkshire people denominate them. In kittlin, the
termination *lin* or *ling*, as seen in duckling, gosling, is
considered a diminutive by some philologists, and a patronymic by others. It is both, for many of the patronymics
are names derived from the father, and, relatively speaking,
a son is little when compared with his father. In the
Anglo-Saxon version of the Gospels, Elisha's servant is
called Elising, as the Roman freedman took the name of
his former master. Thus Marcipor was the boy *(puer)* of
Marcius ; and even at the present day a Southern States
proprietor speaks of his slave as his boy, whatever be his
age. From the patronymic *ing, lin,* we derive such names
as Banting, Branding, where the meaning was originally all
of the family of Brands. So, too, Johnson, Thomson, &c.,
were once John's son, &c., the same as the Norman-French
Fitz and the Russian *Vitch*—Fitzclarence, Czarovitch.
The early English used the word Childe to denote this, as
Childe Elle, Childe Waters ; and Byron had the old notion,
too, when he wrote his grand poem *Childe Harold.* The
Danes in the Danelagh, *i.e.,* land north of the Humber,
applied the word barn in the same way.

Canute had divided England into four great earldoms, each ruled,
under him, by a jarl, or earl ; a Danish, not a Saxon title.

At his death in 1036 the earldoms of Northumbria and East Anglia—
the more strictly Danish parts—were held by a true Danish hero,
Siward Biorn, alias *Digre,* " the Stout," conqueror of Macbeth and
son of the Fairy Bear ; proving his descent, men said, by his pointed
and hairy ears.

It is but probable, nevertheless, that Hereward, as the only man
among the fugitives who ever showed any ability whatsoever, and who
was also the only leader (save Morcar) connected with the fen, con-
ceived the famous " Camp of Refuge," and made it a formidable fact.
Be that as it may, Edwin and Morcar went to Ely, and there joined
an Earl Tosti (according to Richard of Ely), unknown to history ; a
Siward *Barn,* " the boy or the chieftain," who had been dispossessed
of lands in Lincolnshire ; and other valiant and noble gentlemen—the
last wrecks of the English aristocracy. And there they sat in Abbot
Thurstan's hall, and waited for Sweyn and the Danes.—*Hereward the
Wake,* c. 25.

That kitlin means to bring forth kitlins (kittens) is much the
same as the Yorkshire kindle, to bring forth young; that is,
to bring forth after its kind. The first syllable of tickle is
akin to touch, tack, take, &c. (see No. 2).

(137.) LUCK, CHANCE, FORTUNE. — *Lykke* (Danish),
Lycka (Swedish). It signified fortune of any kind, like the
French *heur;* but now it seems to imply good fortune, as
may be seen in the word lucky. Luki was the evil being
chained till the appearing of the twilight of the gods,[*]
according to the Scandinavian Mythology; and when he is
unchained, the world will be at an end. This *heur* (luck)
is distinct from *heure* (hour), and is another form of *aür*
(Provençal), a syncopation of *augur* (Latin), or *av-garr* or
avisgarrit, the bird talks. It is written in English ure and
hour (not time). " The pleasant spring straight draweth
in ure."—*Surrey.* " And wisdom willed me without pro-
tract, in speedi wise to put the same in ure."—Sackville's
Gordubac. " She put her will in ure."—*Surrey. Bonaür*
and *malaür* (Provençal), *bonheur* and *malheur.* These
words came to be spelt with an *h* from the confusion in
men's minds that a connection existed between augury and
astrology, between wishing one well *(heureux)*, and drawing
one's horoscope. The confusion exists also in English,
and it is difficult at times to distinguish between hour
(time), and hour (luck). For instance : " What hour is it?"
is time; you " come at a good hour," is luck. " Me
destine, my fate, and hour I bliss " (luck).—Chaucer's
Court of Love. Lawk-a-day is an exclamation of wish for
luck. *Alack-hap*, from the Welsh, is luck-chance. Chancy
is from *chéance* (French), falling by accident, means by
falling, and an unexpected fortune is called a windfall,
borrowed from the wind blowing fruit off trees. Like luck,
hour, and fortune, hap generally means good fortune, as
is seen in happy, haply. " Right as his happy day "—
Chaucer's *Troylus and Cryseide.* " The happes ouer
mannes hede been honged with a tender threde."—*Gower.*
With vagueness annexed we have hap, happen, *i.e.*, per

---

[*] In German, Göttesdammerung sounds like swearing, doesn't it?
—operatised by Wagner.

chance, by chance, per case, from *per casum* or *cadere*, to fall. "As it fell upon a day."—*Shakespeare*. With a bad sense we have mishap, unhappy, hapless. " And sheld hem fro unhappe."—Chaucer's *House of Fame*. Round Halifax they use *ashelt* for perhaps ; and round Leeds it is *mebby* (may be), like the French *peut-être* and the German *es mag sein*. In Old English it is belike. " Belike you mean to make a puppet of me."—Shakespeare's *Taming of the Shrew*. " Belike through impotence."—*Milton*. Be-like means by luck, and in Westmoreland it is mappen, *i.e.*, may happen ; and Chaucer writes it uphap.—Vide his *Test of Love* (book I.). Peradventure implies chance, on the principle of " nothing venture nothing have." Of the Romanic stock of words that have kinship with words of prediction from birds there are auspices and auguries, the functions of the soothsayers of the one being merged in process of time into those of the other. " *Dant operam simul auspicio augurüsque.*"—*Ennius*. The soothsayer was consulted previous to any undertaking—Virgil's *George III.*, 486—and at a marriage he was considered the " best man." He was called *nuptiarum auspex*, and in Greek *Parangmphios* or, as in St. John, iii, 29 : *Philos tod nymphion*. In *Samson Agonistes*, line 1020, Milton uses the very word *paranymph*. His duty nowadays seems to be to augur the best fortune to the *cari sposi*. Abominate meant nothing more than to deprecate an omen, " *absit omen*," or as we say, " God forbid." *Dio me ne guardi, Tolga Iddio*. Thus the French " *à la bonne heure*," as an encouragement ; in Latin, "*quod faustum felixque sit;*" in German, "*unberufen;*" in Italian, " *magara;*" all seem to give a notion of depreca-tion of danger, *i.e.*, abominable, where a person is boasting of some advantage he possesses ; and the answer might be like Mr. Croaker's " Heaven send we be all no worse this day six months."—*Goldsmith*. Disaster, ill-starred, lunatic, moonstruck, planetstruck, aspect, in the ascendant, dismal, *i.e.*, *dies malus* (Latin), sinister or ominous, from the *augur* prognosticating on the left side of the bird's entrails, are all of astrological source, and are *trita et obvia ;* besides a host of others exclusively applied to that exploded science : assextile, quartile, trine, conjoined, houses, cusps, astonish,

astound, astonnied *(Bible)*, *étonné* (French), eccentric, lunes.
"Your husband is at his old lunes again."—*Merry Wives
of Windsor.* " I scorn their lunes."—*The Purgatory of
Suicides.* Consider means look at the stars. For a beautiful use of this word turn to viii. Psalm, and then admit
the thorough appropriateness of the English translation of
the Scriptures. In Horatio's speech, on seeing the ghost,
is a life-like description of the planetary influence. Milton,
too, in *Paradise Lost*, vi. "My stars," however, as an oath, is
an abbreviation of " My stars and garters," alluding to the
Order of the Garter. As a soldier would swear by his
sword, so a noble would by his garter ; and in fact Goldsmith hints at this in his *Vicar of Wakefield.*

(138.) SAD, applied to a potato, is in apposition to floury
or mealy potato. Rev. W. Gaskell says this word is in use
in Lancashire, and derived from the Welsh *sad,* meaning
firm. To me it seems to be another form of the word
sodden, watery, and derived from the Anglo-Saxon *sadian,*
to wet, and is then connected with seethe, suds, and sot,
one whose clay is well *soaked.* Let's hev a gill o' yale.

(139.) POSNIT, an iron pan. Set-pot, what Londoners
term a copper for washing clothes. *Rekon,* the perforated
iron bar, having a hooked end, from which is suspended
the *posnit.* This *rekon* is called in Norfolk a *spirket.*

(140.) KENSPACK, possessing a marked peculiarity. *Ken-
speckle* (Scotch) is some mark by which a person is peculiarly
distinguished from another ; as one would say, " I should
know him again amongst a thousand."

(141.) LEADEATER, indiarubber, which by rubbing eats
out the lead pencil marks.

(142.) BEC is a brook ; *bec* (Anglo-Saxon), *bœck* (Danish),
das bach (German). This word is found in Wansbeckwater,
where

Danish.	*Gaelic.*	*A. Saxon.*	*English.*
Wand——	s ——	beck——	water.
Wand——	uisge——	beck——	water.

Here all four words mean water. The explanation is that
each tribe, forgetting the meaning, added its own word.
Holbeck near Leeds, in Yorkshire, and Holbeck

in Schleswig; London on the Thames in Canada and in Middlesex; Plaistow near Bromley in Kent and in Essex;—these present curious connections in the history of languages depending on migration. Nic. Grimoald (A.D. 1542) calls the Icarian Sea a *beck*.

> Icar, with fire hadst thou the midway known.
> Icarian *Beck* by name had no man Inown (y-known).

Look thou there where Wrigglesby *Beck* comes out by the hill.— Tennyson's *Northern Farmer.*

In some parts it is bach, as in Sandbach.

Some Yorkshire words may be considered present English, but in which, however, the pronunciation slightly differs. In certain instances this dialectic variation of pronunciation is older than ordinary English. A Yorkshireman myself, I may say with Dante, *"Fabbro del parlar materno" (Purg.* xxvi, 117). Many of these words are bright, like stars in the sky, and it is a pity they should be allowed to "swim beyond our ken." A dialect in Italy is spoken by *all* in that district, rich and poor, low and high; but an English dialect, alas! is confined to the lower classes, and held in such disesteem that many consider it as English mispronounced. But at one time this was not so : the gentry spoke the dialect of their locality—for a dialect was a language. Queen Elizabeth's Court spoke pretty broad Wessex, and the gentlemen of the North kept up the Scandinavian, as did those of the West country the western dialects. According to Isaac D'Israeli *(Am. of Lit.,* p. 241) the Duchess of Norfolk (one of the most accomplished ladies of the 16th century, the friend of scholars and the patron of literature) wrote to the Earl of Essex :—" My ffary gode lord, her I send you in tokyn hoff the new eyer, a glasse of setyl set in sellfer gyld. I pra you tak hit wort. An hy wer habel het showlde be bater. I woll hit war wort a. m. crone." This is in the peasant dialect of Hants, Surrey and Middlesex. The *a. m. crone* means a thousand crowns.

(143.) SEN for *self* and *selves,* in composition with my, his, thy, her, &c., as me-sen, wer-sen, her-sen, &c. This is certainly regular, which the English is not, as self is sometimes added to the personal pronouns, and sometimes to the reciprocals. To be consistent we ought to say his-self and theirselves, as we do in myself and ourselves. Some of the old writers actually have this form. "Every of us, each for *hisself*, laboured how to receive him."—*Sidney.* "That they would willingly and of *theirselves* endeavour to keep a perpetual chastity."—*2nd and 3rd statute Edward VI.*, c. 21. It is observable that when these pronouns are parted by the word *own* they become regular. About London the common people have mine, thine, hissen, hern, ourn, yourn. This form is also old, for I find in the *Revelation to the Monk of Evesham*, xxviii, c. (A.D. 1189), "A certain neighbour of herns." The Anglo-Saxon for reflection annexed *sylf* (self), and for possession *agen* (own); and most likely the London *hern* and *yourn* are amalgamations of her own, your own, &c., as the German dative; while the Yorkshire his-sen, me-sen, &c., are corruptions for *self*. A circus jester had not been very well received at Barnsley, so taking this mild method of sarcasm, he told his audience that the mayor dying, his soul went up to heaven's gate and knocked. St. Peter put his head through the wicket and asked : "Who's thear?" "It's me." "Who's me, an' whear dusta cum thro'?" "Aa cum fro Bairnsley an' Aa'm t' mayor : so Aa want ta cum in." "Tha can't, my lad; beside, Aa don't knaw Bairnsley. Whearabats is it?" "Bairnsley! wha ivrybody knaws Bairnsley, the birthplace of the gert Tommy Treddlehoile." "Aa can't let tha in. Niver herd tell on it. Nobody iver comes to heaven fro that place, so tak the *sen* off." Self (English) becomes *sen* in South Yorkshire, and *sel* in the North.

> They turn round like grindlestones,
> Which they dig out *fro'* the dells
> For their *bairns* bread, wives and *sells*.
>   —*Ben Jonson.*

(144.) WAR for worse, in Danish *værre*, is a regular comparative, which was probably declined woe, war, warst. So it was in the Anglo-Saxon. As for bad, badder, baddest, this is very *bad* indeed; but Chaucer had badder; and Shakespeare is *worse* still, for he wrote worser. I am not trying to be witty. Some years ago I heard a man at Lightcliffe say : "Fratchin's bad enough, bud feightin's *war*."

pun and truth (see No. 52). It is odd that in English the words worse, less, and near, although the real comparatives of bad, little, and nigh, are dealt with as adjectives in the positive degree, and a second set of comparatives are formed, viz., worser, lesser, and nearer.

(145.) NOR, for than : " I will end heir, lest my preface be langer *nor* my purpose and haill mater following."—King James I. *Phœnix.*

(146.) OPPEN, for open (German *offen*), *watter* for water (German *wasser*), are nearer the German than the English sound ; whilst ommost for almost, nobbut for not but (or only), and many more follow the classic system of softening the former of two consonants for euphony, as oppose, pellucid, illegal, instead of obpose, perlucid, inlegal. Mak for make (German *mache*), wakken for awaken (German *wachen*), spak, in Scotch, for spoke (German *sprache*),* spokken for spoken (German *gesprochen*), are also more like the German in the vowel-sound, and shoemakker is exactly the German *schuhmacher ;* so are brek for break (German *breche*), brokken for broken (German *gebrochen*).

(147.) DRUKKEN for drunken loses the *n.* In Norwegian this is also the case. Drukkenbolt being a sot, a fill-pot ; and in Danish *drikke* is to drink.

(148.) NOBBUT, for only, is an amalgamation of *not but:* " For he's nobbut a curate."—Tennyson's *Northern Farmer.* In that witty ballad, *The Yorkshire Horse Dealer,* made so popular by the fine singing of Emery, it occurs :

> And if Tommy I nobbut can happen to trap,
> It 'll be a fine feather i' Aberram cap.

In reference to the last two words of this couplet, it is worthy of note that Yorkshire folks never put the sign of the possessive where the relative substantive immediately follows ; but if it be understood and not expressed the *s* is inserted. For instance, quoting from the same ballad,

> But 'twor Tommy opinion, he'd dee on himsel,

illustrates the former, and

---

* Can any one tell me how the *r* crept in Sprechen ? It has intruded in gi*r*l, brideg*r*oom, la*r*k, &c. (See No. 45.)

> Hee'd a horse, too, 'twor war nor oud Tommy's,

explains the latter. It is curious that our Anglo-Saxon
fathers did the same with feminine nouns; we still say
Lady day (not Lady's-day), but in the masculine the Lord's
day. Again, look at lady-bird.

(149.) Lop is a flea. *Loppe* (Danish) from the word
loup, to jump, is just as expressive as flea, from flee.*

* Life is sweet, as t' flee said when it tummeld into t' treacle.

"Spak o' loupin' ower a lynn," writes Burns in his *Duncan
Gray.* "Syr Cauline *loup'd* from care-bed soone."— *Old
Ballad.* In the same way the insect fly is with us a flee,
as butterfly is butterflee, the very sound of flea. It is so spelt
in Drayton's *Nymphidia,* "The wing of a pied butterflee."
Spenser wrote his earliest pieces at Hurstwood, near Burn-
ley. As being "master of our northern dialect," says
Dryden, "his *Shepherd's Kalendar*" teems with phrases and
words that are current north of the Humber. Lop for leap,
afore for before, wark for work or ache, from wœrc (Anglo-
Saxon) pain, and a whole host besides indicate this. Skelton
(temp. Henry VIII.) writes :

> Of Triston and King Marke,
> And all the whole wark,
> Of Bel I sold his wife.

Bellywark, in English is stomach ache, gripes, or the working of the guts (Borborygm). Ben Jonson uses *wark,* so
does Lord Vaux, A.D. 1531. La grippé (French) has nothing to do with the gripes ; it is the influenza.

> Methinks I hear the clerk
> That knolls the careful knell,
> And bids me leave my woeful *warke,*
> Ere nature me compel.
>
> Of yellow tabtais was hir sark
> Begaryit all with browderit *wark,*

i.e., "Her shift was of yellow taffeta, and ornamented with
broidered work."—Sir David Lindsay (died 1557, A.D.,) in
his *Squyre Meldrum.* The "Brafforth" joker told his
friend who had the stomach ache, "Thaa'l niver want
summat ta dew while the belly *warks* for tha." A Yorkshireman applies this *wark* to belly, but never uses it in
tooth-ache, ear-ache, and head-ache.

(150.) Aboon for above :

> And bending higher David's lute in tone,
> With courage seke your endles crowne *abone*.
> —King James I., *Essaye of a Prentice, &c.*, 1589.

(151.) Wor for was follows the German *ich war*, I was. " Doänt thee marry for money, but goa where money is : an a went where money *war*."—Tennyson's *Northern Farmer*. This *wor* serves for all the three persons and both numbers, whereas in the Anglo-Saxon it was : ic wæs, thu wære, he wæs, we wæron, &c.

(152.) Awther and Nawther are found so written as far back as the 12th century. A story is told of two disputants who, referring to a Yorkshire schoolmaster as to the correct pronunciation of this word, whether *yther* or *eether*, received the answer " Awther 'll du," thus unconsciously giving a third sound. The modes of pronouncing these words seem to differ in each town of Yorkshire. I have heard neither, nyther, nayther, nowther, nawther, &c. *Nathor* was the Anglo-Saxon spelling.

(153.) Owt and Nowt, for anything or nothing, are akin to aught and nought. " Parson's lass ant nowt, an she weant ha' nowt when he's dead." " The bees is as fell as owt."—Tennyson's *Northern Farmer*.

(154.) Thro', for *from*, was originally fro, and still survives in the expression " to and fro." " And alle his people he reysegd were fledde *fro* hym."— *Warksworth Chronicle* (temp. Edward IV.) " Afore this Aa used to borra money *thro* Tom." " When Aa cam hoam *thro* my wark." As *through* (English), from beginning to end, and *thro* (Yorks.), distance, either space or time, sound alike, many are the Yorkshire jokes equivocal. Ex. gr. " Aa can push that hat *thro* this wedding ring." He puts his finger *through* the ring and pushes the hat. " I can push this hat *thro*' the wall ! " He pushes it away *from* the wall.

(155.) Fayther and father (rhymes with lather), muther, doughter, follow the old writers.

> Farewell my doughter Katherine, late the fere,
> To Prince Arthur myne own chyld so dere.
> —*Sir Thomas More.*

G

The vowel sounds are more Continental than English. For
instance, *a* is the French *a ; e* in such words as sir, her,
is a short sound approaching the French *eu* in *peur ; o* is
the Italian *o* when followed by a double consonant ; and *u*
is the Italian *u* or the English *oo* in food, though at times
it comes nearer the *ew* in our word few.

(156.) OWER for over ; mony for many.

> By crossing ower to mony countrys.
> —King James I. *Phœnix.*

Give ower means be quiet.

(157.) ONY for any. In a Patent Roll, anno 43, Henry
III., mem. xv, No. 40, I find, "And gif *oni*, other *onie*
cumen her ongenes, we willen and heaten thæt alle ure
treowe heom healden deadliche," which Somner translates
by "*Sive vir sive fœmina.*" The whole passage is : "If *any
man* or *any woman* come here against (our permission, is
understood) we will and order that all our true men hold them
deadly." One of Caxton's advertisements, 1490 A.D., begins
"If it please *ony* man spirituel or temporel," &c.

(158.) KNAW for know.

> It gives him dayis his God aright to knaw.
> —King James I. *Tyme.*

Hunter, V.P., of Battersea College, remarked one day to a
student of the name of Glasse, who was rather short-
tempered, "You should not be so brittle, or you may
crack." "Aah doan't knaw what you mean," replied Glasse.
"Come," said the vice-principal, "try a joke ; make a *retort*, Mr.
Glasse." The laboratory pun made us all smile, a kind of
nictitation, Wynkyn de Worde (winking at the word).

(159.) WHITTLE means a clasp knife : the word is used
in South Yorkshire, hwytel (Anglo-Saxon). It was
taken over to America by the Pilgrim Fathers,
where many English words are found that are
obsolete in England. The Yankee (of caricature) is
nothing without his hickory stick, which he whittles whilst
talking. The word is seen in *whet*, to sharpen, to pare off ;
and it is derived from hwitel (Anglo-Saxon), a pocket knife.
Chaucer in his *Canterbury· Pilgrims* says : " A Sheffield
whittle bare he in his hose," which shows that Sheffield

even then (15th century) was noted for its cutlery, and that
knives were worn in the stocking, like the skean-dhu of the
Gael. In Hispano-America the Gaucho of the Pampas
wears such a knife (cuchillo) in his big jack boots (botazas).
If anyone likes to call he can see the one I wore when I
was in the Gran Chaco. Shakespeare mentions the word in
Timon of Athens, v. 2 ; it is also in *Tim Bobbin :* " But the
dule o' th' whittle wur t' be leet on."

> And syne bring here a sharpening stane,
> We'll sharp our whittles ilka ane.

From the *New Year's Ditty* in the Orkneys, which I have
slightly modernised. In the old ballad of the *Boy and the
Mantle* (Percy's *Reliques*) I found :

> When thrice he over the boar's head,
> His little wand had drawne,
> Quoth he, " There's never a cuckold's knife
> Can carve this head of brawne."
> Then some their whittles rubbed,
> On whetstone and on hone," &c.

DIALOGUE.—Cockney : " What hev you got there, my man ?"
Pudsey man : " Two whittles."
Cockney : "Then you'll never be out of grub, cos you've got yer
whittles (victuals)—see ?

Akin to *whittle*, the woodpecker is the wetel (Bucks), and
woodwale (Chaucer), widwael (Belgian), woodwell (old
ballad). Woodspite, hew-hole, woodpecker, refer to peck-
ing, as pick-a-tree (old English), picchio (Italian), picama-
deros (Spanish). The French pivert refers to the tapping,
reminding one of Tom Moore's "woodpecker tapping at
the hollow beech tree."

(160.) MOULD, for might, is analogically like would, could,
should, both in spelling and pronunciation. It has a better
right to a grammatical position than *could*. *Would* and
should are evidently conjugational inflections of *will* and
shall ; but *could* is erroneously formed from *can :* its old
form was *couth*. If the English *can* by a false analogy
becomes *could*, why should not the Yorkshire make a
similar mistake with *may* and *mould*.

English.	*Yorkshire.*
will, would	will, would
shall, should	sall, sould
can, could	can, could
may, might	may, mould

all pronounced to rhyme with good. The L in should was once pronounced as seen in the ballad *Boy and the Mantle*, thus shewing its kinship with shall :

> When thus she had her shriven,
> And her worst fault had told,
> The mantle soon became her,
> Right comely as it *shold*.

(161.) CAPT. " Aa'm fairly capt " is " I'm really puzzled in the head " (caput, Latin). In the Milanese dialect there is a parallel word mentecatt, meaning bewildered, from mente, the mind ; captus, taken prisoner ; tonto, in Spanish.

(162.) PEGGY is the wooden three-legged hand-worker for turning about the dirty linen in the wash tub. In London it is the "dolly." Never mind: Margaret and Mary are cousins.

(163.) GUTTLING and GUZZLING have been formed by jingling assonance. Guttling, connected with gutta (Latin), a drop ; or perhaps from the vulgar way of saying " filling your guts." Guzzling, from gosier (French), the throat. So the phrase seems to mean eating inordinately and drinking sottishly, the exact opposite to the refined gourmands et gourmets (French). Guttlers and guzzlers would very well describe our Anglo-Saxon ancestors, while gourmands and gourmets would apply to the Normans.

(164.) PATTENS are wood-soled clogs standing on iron rings, and used in wet weather. In French there is Patin for a dish or plate, like the Latin Patina, as in " Patinas cœnabat omasi."—*Horace, Epist. i, xv, 34*, of which the diminutive was patella ; and in the Milanese dialect padella is a frying pan.

> Look how the floor of heaven
> Is thick inlaid with *patines* of bright gold.
> —*Merchant of Venice*, v, i.

Where Lorenzo alludes to the innumerable stars like flat discs. Milton in his *Comus* (649) speaks of the " dull swain with his clouted shoon." Some commentators think this refers to the iron rings on his shoes, others to the hobnails, because (clou, French for a nail) we have the phrase " clout nails." N.B.—Clout, · a rag, is another word altogether.

(165.) THE STATTERS or HIRING FAIR which are established by law, that is by *statutes*, when boys and girls stand in rows to be hired as labourers and servants like the German Kermesse. You can see the girls in the "Cloches de Corneville" where they are singing "Look at that, and look at this, I don't think I am amiss." A young woman at Helmsley told me "We 'r cal'd statters 'cos we stand like statters." I smiled at the confusion between statutes and statues—right to a "T"!

(166.) SWARM in English means a multitude, a throng of bees, men or anything; but in Yorkshire it means to climb. "At the top was placed a piece of money, as a prize for those who could swarm up and seize it."—Coxe's *Russia*.

(167.) To JOWL, to knock a person's head against a wall, or two people knocking their heads together.

> And gave that reverend head a mall
> Of one or two against the wall (Butler's *Hudibras*),

would be "He jowled his head again 't wall."

> And his head, as he fell,
> Went nickety-nock,
> Like a pebble in Carisbrooke Well.
> Horace Smith's *Rejected Addresses*.

(168.) DICKEY-BIRD is from dicken (Welsh), meaning a hen-bird. It sounds catachrestic, dickey for a hen, as we usually take Robin Redbreast, Jackass, Billy-goat, &c., for males.

(169.) CHILDER is correct, while the English children is not, the *r* being a relic of one form of the Anglo-Saxon plural, and the *en* a second form of another plural: thus children is a double plural.

> Welcome, brother, to kyn and kythe
> Thi wife and childer that come the with.
> —*Towneley Mysteries*.

And a Christmas carol gives the penultimate accent, shewing the two plurals:

> God bless the master of this house,
> Likewise the mistress too,
> And all the little *childeren*
> That round about them go.

(170.) Doy is the diminutive of *darling*, which darling is again the diminutive of *dear*. Its origin I do not know. About 1577 a mystery-play was enacted in Chester, and one part, De Deluvio Noë, was assigned to the good simple Waterleaders and Drawers of the Dee (the river), no doubt with a humourous sense of appropriateness to their calling : this play ends by God saying

> My blessing now I give thee here,
> To thee, Noë, my servant *dear* ;
> For vengeance shall no more appear,
> And now farewell, my *darling dear*.

Here the double endearment with another rhyming dear would all be expressed by the Yorkshire *doy ;* just as tender is the Spanish *querido*, the Italian *carino*, or the Scotch *dearie.*

"The development at the back of the head, my friends, indicates parental affection," explained the phrenologist. "Now you will observe," he went on, feeling the head of the boy on the platform, "that this bump is abnormal in size, thus indicating that this lad loves and reveres his parents to an unusual degree. Is that not so, my lad ?"

"Noa, it isn't."

"You do not love your parents ?"

"Wha mi muther's mi *doy*, bud me fayther, noa. That bump o' mi heäd he ga' mi this morning wi his crooch."

This word is probably a softened form of joy. I knew an old woman in Wilsden who used to say "Come to the mammy, joy."—Æthelbert Binns.

(171.) Whist. Ho'd thee whist, means keep silence. The English phrase, "Hold your noise," seems reasonable, but the Yorkshire "Ho'd the whisht," or hold your silence, is whimsical. This word is "The wild waves whist" of Shakespeare's *Ariel*, and Milton's "The winds with wonder whist" *Hymn of the Nativity*. It is also in whist, a game of cards, which requires more silence and less talk.

(172.) Midge (in English a Gnat) is from the Anglo-Saxon myge, in modern German die Mücke. So small an insect, its name midge gives us the word midget for anything diminutive.

> In corneris and clere fenesteris of glas
> Full besely Arachne wevand was,
> To knit hyr nettis and hyr wobbis slee
> Therewith to cauch the litil *mige* or flee.
>   —*Gawin Douglas* (died 1522).

The *midges* dance aboon the burn.—*R. Tannahill.*

Our Anglo-Saxon ancestors had *myge* (a midge), *gnæt* (gnat) and *hnitu* (nit), the egg of very small animals. There is no doubt that there was a reactionary connection between gnat and nit. This troublesome pest has a *cousin* all over the world, in France, le cousin (see the joke?), in Italy zanzara, from its buzzing; in Spain mosquito or the little fly (mosca). Is a *Nat*uralist one who catches g*nats*? Now, you Entomological Societies.

(173.) CUSHIE-COW-LADY is the ladybird, and, as a favourite of all children, has a name in most countries which refers to something holy: ex. gr. in English ladybird, our Lady the Virgin Mary; in German das Gotteskühchen, God's little cow; like the French bête-à-dien, God's beast; in Spanish mariquita, little Virgin Mary. The Spaniards also call it vaca de San Anton, Saint Antony's cow; and vaquita de San Anton, Saint Antony's little cow. In the United States it is termed ladycow, and as all beetles there are bugs this pretty coccinella (Italian) is the ladybug (see No. 70). Can any friend inform me why this little pet is a bird, a beast, a bug, a cow, a lady? Why a she? Is it on the Norfolk principle, where they call everything a *he*, except a Tom-cat, and that they call a *she*?

(174.) MOLDYWARP is the Mole, from the Gothic der maul, the snout. This little animal is der Maulwurf in German. In some parts of Yorkshire it is named want, from the old Danish wand, in Norwegian vond, to go. The Welsh name is gwadd and twrch daear. In the Romance tongues it is talpa (Latin), la taupe (French), la talpa (Italian), el topo (Spanish), toupiero (Portuguese), by reason "terram fodiens."

(175.) FATTY-CAKE is round flat bread made with butter, dripping or saim: by some it is called short-cake. The London spice-loaf is in Yorkshire spice cake. To cake is the word for the hissing of geese, just as for hens we say to cackle. Baff (another expressive Yorkshire word) means the suppressed bark of a dog, the ghost of a sound.

(176.) INUFF means enough. A mother, speaking of a fatty-cake, observed "Aa think it's dun tew much." The

husband, looking round at his large family and then at the
small cake, drily answered, " Nay, 'lass, Aa doan't think it's
inuff."

(177.) TEEM, to rain in torrents. Tyman (Anglo-Saxon)
to bring forth, but in English it means to bring forth anything largely.

> Fancy with prophetic glance
> Sees the teeming months advance."
> —T. Warton's *Spring*.

> Heaven's youngest—teemed star.
> —Milton's *Hymn of the Nativity*.

> Belike for want of rain, which I could well
> Beteem them from the tempest of mine eyes.
> —*Midsummer Night's Dream*, i, 1.

In Yorkshire we say " It teems wi' rain," and I never heard
it applied to anything else.

(178.) TO PUT YORKSHIRE ON A MAN, is to cheat, to
best a man as they say in London. " Has ta naw heard ot
tat creawse tike ha donn'd oytch on um a bantling eh three
o' the kest-off jumps, and think'nt put Yorshar o' fok?"—
Tim Bobbin's Lancashire Dialect. Again, a gentleman,
praising the ostler of the inn who had displayed uncommon
cuteness, remarked, " You have plenty of perquisites here,
and as you're so sharp, and a Yorkshireman too, I wonder
you've not yet made your fortune." Said the man : "An so
Aa su'd, but t' maister 's Yorkshire tew, an' Aa can't put
Yorksher on him." I really cannot say why the phrase of
putting Yorkshire on a man should signify chousing a chap,
monkeying a man, fooling a fellow, kidding a cove, when it
is acknowledged by all thinking people that Yorkshire folks
are the most honest and free from guile* of any class in
England.

(179.) NEAR Bridlington, one wet morning, some fisher
folks with a basket of flithers (limpets), observing some
ducklings, remarked " 'Twhat maks 'em pick 'em?" A
gentleman hearing this said to his servant: "Your'e Scotch;
now what does that mean?" The servant replied : " Aa
dinna ken : 'tis nae Scotland, it's Yorkshire ; but may be
A'l speer." On enquiry it turned out that it meant " What
makes the ducklings plume themselves?"

---

* Like Nathaniel.

(180.) CHIMLEY for chimney is used north of the Humber. In Leeds there's a nursery rhyme :

> Chimley sweeper, blackymoor,
> Set o' t' top o' t' chapel door,
> Tak a stick an' knock him daan ;
> That's the way to Chapeltaan.

Il cammino (Italian), *la cheminée* (French), *das Kamin* (German), *la cheminea* (Spanish), all refer to *way :* the chimney is the *way* out for the smoke. There was no Anglo-Saxon word for chimney, because they had no such thing. The fire was on the hearth, and the smoke got out where it could, or it didn't get out at all.

(181.) CROOKELT means awry, crooked, from *cric* (Anglo-Saxon). There was an old English word, *acroke*, which signified *awkward*. The Yorkshire crookelt is akin to *kreukelen* (Dutch), *krökle* (Norwegian), and *krukeln* (Platt Deutsch).

(182). RIVE, to tear clothes ; but in English it is to split, to rend anything. " Tha'll rive thee frock if tha doesn't luke aat." Anglo-Saxon *ryft*, Swedish *rifva*, Danish *river*. Rift is a cleft. It is curious that this last word (in *cleave)* has the catachrestic meanings of detaching and attaching, like *let*, to permit, and let, to *hinder*. Hamlet cries " *Let* me go : by heavens I'll make a ghost of him that *lets* me."

(183.) TO LEET ON means to alight on, to settle upon, to come across a thing or person. " Aa couldn't leet on him, tho' Aa luked aboon hauf an hour i' Morgan's yard." Alight, to settle upon and alight to kindle have no derivational affinity. *Alight*, to settle on, was the *alihtan* (A. Saxon), *lichten* (Dutch), *sich niederlassen, absteigen* (German). *Alight*, to kindle, was *alcoht, aliht* (A. Saxon), *licht, leuchten* (German).

(184.) READAMADEASY, the little book, the *Reading Made Easy* given to children after they have mastered the alphabet, something like the old-fashioned *Hornbook* which was covered with a slice of horn in a frame to keep it neat, and without being dog's-eared. This *Reading Made Easy* and the *Hornbook* began with the alphabet : and the latter in the catholic days of England had a cross in front of the A B C and the child made the sign of the cross before repeating, so that it was named the Christ-cross-row. When I was teacher in a Spanish College at Montevideo I noticed that the order to say the letters was " Digame el Cristo A.B.C." The Spanish poet Camacho alludes to this in his *A mi hijita de cinco años*. Prior alludes, in a whimsical way, to this *Hornbook :*—

> To master Iohn, the English maid,
> A hornbook gives of gingerbread :
> And that the child may learn the better,
> As he can name, he eats a letter.

(185.) ANPASSAL is the finish of the alphabet, and means, I suppose, *and parcel*, or (though not generally known) the English *amperzand :* at least *Punch* said so in one of his numbers. It is the symbol, &c., which is the result of rapidly writing *etc. (et cætera)* as & is of et. English, And so on ; and so forth. French, Et comme ça ; Et ainsi de suite. German, Und so weiter. Italian, E così via via ; C; osì E via dicendo. Spanish, Y así de lo demas. Latin, Et cætera.

(186.) TOM-SPINNER is the daddy-long-legs.

Tak thi long legs off t' harstone. Thaa'rt like a tom-spinner, flingin' 'em abaat as if they didn't belong to tha."—*B. Preston*.

(187.) To SAM is to gather ; *sammeln* (German), and is related to *sum*, meaning to add, and *some*, the partitive adjective, the root of which is found in many languages : the Latin derived it from their Gothic invaders *(sumo*, I gather).

> For all their battels *samyn* were in a schiltrum.
> —Barbour's *Bruce*, vol. ii,

meaning "All the soldiers were massed in a heap." To *sam* is used also in Devonshire.

(188.) LOPPERED means stained (see No. 149.)

Tha'l mucky thi stocking-feet wi' soot an' black leäd : Aa'v often wondered whot made t' bed sheets so *loppard*, bud Aa see it's thee 'at does it wi' goin to bed wi' thi stockins full o' coil dust an' all maks o' muck.—*B. Preston*.

(189.) THREE-THRUMS, the purring of a cat, is to my seeming very expressive of the sound indi*cat*ing content-ment, and certainly more so than the German *schnurren*.

The Scotch gray-thrums is also onomatopean.

> Hey, Willie Winkie, are ye coming ben ?
> The cat's singing *grey thrums* to the sleeping hen ;
> The dog's spelder'd on the floor, and disna gi'e a cheep ;
> But here's a waukrife laddie that winna fa' asleep.
> — *W. Miller*, 1810.

Other nations seem to have nothing shorter than a peri-phrase. Spanish—El susurro de los gatos cuando están contentos. French — Filer comme le chat. Italian — Fremito del gatto quando accarezza.

(190.) MAISTER is a word of compellation. "Oh maister ! yer boot's loise."

(191.) NIVER HEED means do not mind.

"Luke, lad, he's makking fun o' tha."
"Wha, niver heed ; it wean't hurt ma."

(192). PILEROW, on old Yorkshire word, meant the list of marks used by printers, such as hyphen, colon, asterisk, comma, &c.

(193.) BADLY OFF is that impecunious state that Tenny-son calls "eternal want of pence," which he copied from the Italian *eterna mancanza di quattrini.* Y yo tambien estoy sin empleado, y por esta razon no tengo plata. Si, Vd. quiere ajudarme, mi harà muy favor.

(194.) PENNY DUCK, called in London faggots, is a cooked mixture of pig's lights and blood, seasoned with herbs. The *Pogmoor Almanack* calls it the "Denarius Ducky-hen-sis !"

(195.) SITHA means *look now, i.e.,* see thou, look there.

(196.) REKKON, to feign, to pretend.

"Let's lake at faythers an muthers. Tom sall be fayther an Aa'l rekkon to be t' muther."

(197.) LIKE means deprecating, mitigating, apologetic.

"If ya give me hauf-a-crown for t' owd kettle, *like,* Aa's sewer ta be content."

"Aa sudden't loik ta cum withaat being axed."
"Ay fur suer, tha can cum as if tha wor just passing, *like.*"

In Leeds the children had a street game in which, among other words, I call to mind :

> Sally made a pudding,
>   Sho made it ower sweet,
> Sho dursn't stick a knife in 't
>   Till *Jack* cam hoam at neet.
> *John*, witta hev a bit, like?
>   Doan't say nay,
> For last Monday morning
>   Was our wedding-day.

Here the difference between Jack away and John at home is the deprecating *like*.   In London there is a similar ditty : the sailor spending his money is John, and having spent his money is Jack.

> Get up, Jack, and let John sit down
> For I see you're outward bound.

It is all the world over " Speed the parting guest, welcome the coming."

(198.) RUD is the West Riding word for a red chalk coloured by the peroxide of iron ; it is called *keel* in Scotland.   In my town it is always termed *red rud*, a duplication of words, as one means the other.   It is used for marking sheep.   The men who dig up this earth are called ruddlemen.

> Besmeared like a ruddleman, a gipsey, or a chimney-sweeper.
> —Burton's *Anatomy of Melancholy*.

In Barnsley it is *ruddal ;* and in Anglo-Saxon *ruddock* was the redbreast, meaning red.   Chaucer writes :

> Her *rudde* is like scarlet in grain.

> Sweet blushes stained her *rud-red* cheeke.
> Percy's *Relics :* " Sir Gawaine."

A *ruddy* countenance is like the Spanish *rubio*.

(199.) SUP means to drink.   " Wita hev a gill o' yale? *sup* lad."   Drinking is that meal called tea,   " Es ta hed thee *drinking* ?"   " Have you had your tea?" or as the French say :   " A notre retour nous five-o'clock-querons à six heures."

(200.) GE'LUKE, about Leeds, the same as *goa luke*, in Barnsley, means get out of it, out of the way, or as the London Coster Girl would say, " Gow on a-why."

(201.) FLAT-IRON is the iron for ironing the clothes in the laundry.

(202.) THE PEACE-EGG, or *pace*, from Paschal, is a play in which the mummers at Easter-tide go about from house to house representing St. George, the Bold Slasher, Little Devil Doubt, and others. In spite of time and place the worthies of all ages are brought together to fight and spout and rant. In the *Yorkshire Magazine* a little sketch of two of these warriors bold had the joke " Peace ? egg," when it is well-known that the word is a misnomer, as everybody kills everybody. At Easter-tide eggs boiled hard and stained of various colours were given to children. At one time the title was " Pase-egg ;" and I recollect a proverb

> Tid, mid, misera
> Carl, Paum, good Pase-day.
> —*Kennett MS.* Lansd. 1033.

(203.) MISSLE. " Chalk an' watter. Som on hem hev a pump agean t' missle." I don't know the word myself.

MISTLE.—This is perhaps from the Angio-Saxon *meox* or *myx* and *stal*, a place.—Atkinson's *Cleveland Glossary* ; so Æthelbert Binns writes to me.

(204.) AGEAN, near to, close by, against. " T' owd man lives *agean* t' Vicar's croft."

(205.) LOISE, to set loose. " After t' factory's *loised*, the hands cam out." " Aa can't cum till schoil *loises*."

(206.) COW-CLAP, vaccine excrement. Cazzan is a cow-clap or dried cow's dung. About Bridlington it was the duty of a female servant on a farm to take up the soft cow's dung in her open hand and clap it on a wall or fence, so that it might *cazzan on ;* when it was dry it would peel off, and was then stored away for fuel.

(207.) COUGHING AN' BARKING is the diaphragmatic, convulsive clamour of a bronchial patient, the sound being an involuntary imitation of obstreperous caninity. What think you of this, sesquipedalian verbiage ? Grenadier words ?

(208.) BADGER, says a contributor to the *Leeds Mercury*,

means to cheapen, to haggle over a bargain, like the deaf old lady :—

" How mooch is thes gaan ?"
" Fifteen shillings."
" Fifty shillings ! Aa'll gi ya thirty."
" Aa said fifteen."
(Louder.)   " Fifteen ! Aa'll gi ya twelve."

Now, I am a Leeds man, and I never heard the word in my life, except as the carnivorous texus, or as the name of a fellow-student at Battersea. It is true there is the English *badger*, which means a pedlar. Would the patoisophile say that the Yorkshire dialect is changing ? Language is ever fluctuating. Old words drop out of existence like stragglers deserting from an army of soldiers on a long march. New words are created, borrowed or stolen, to suit the exigencies of philosophy, art or science, like an actor who doubles a part. Some words shift their meanings, like ships that drift from their moorings. Other words, having two or three shades of signification, lose some and retain others, like John Jones Esquire abroad is plain Jack at home. So it is with this greater disadvantage : language, being oral and printed, is almost stereotyped ; whilst dialects, on the contrary, being spoken only, as trade and commerce multiply, rail and road increase, the rapidity of intercommunication gradually eliminates them, like clodhopper Giles of the country becomes in London Mr. Egidius. For instance : the very dialect of the Cockneydom of *Pickwick* has vanished, and a strange combination of scheny Jewish, with the argot of Whitechapel and the nasality of the coster-girl, has taken its place. Folklore, to the lorist, may preserve it on paper, like flies in amber, but as a spoken tongue the speech of Sam Weller is defunct, as Cornish or Erse. So all dialects are dying. Perhaps it explains the difference between that Yorkshire of 1840 and this of 1890.

(209.) GILL, in English is quarter-of-a-pint, in Yorkshire it is half-a-pint. A Londoner never asks for a gill, and a Yorkshireman never for half-a-pint. " Ger hoam wi' tha, thaa foil ! Aa tell tha t' maister's such a nipskin that he wod n't gi' tha a gill of ale, noà—not if his pocket wor full on hem." Rather confusing, is it not ?

(210.) ON STRAP means on credit, or as it is termed in London *on tick*, that is, on the ticket (at my uncle's, I suppose).* Why, on strap?

(211.) SNECK, a latch, is connected with snatch (as make, match; bake, batch; &c.). *Snacken* (Dutch), *schnappen* (German), *snacken* (Teutonic) are all related. *Sneck* is also a Scotch word.

(212.) SPELL OF A CHAIR, the rail, the bar, the round of a ladder, the rung of a ship, which in ship-building is one of the slips of wood to strengthen the deck. Spill in a tap-room is a piece of wood with which to light pipes, and spell in the foot is a splinter.

> Crack nature's mould, all germs *spill* at once
> That make ungrateful man.—*Shakespeare.*

Here poor "Lear" means spill (cludo), shut up, not spill (fundo) pour out like spilt milk, like Gen. xxxviii. 9.

(213.) SOFT, that part of bread in distinction to crust, is thus particularised:

Yorkshire—	crust.	soft.	old.	fresh.
Cockney—	crust.	crumby.	stale.	new.

Bread, the staff of life, has become the general for all comestibles, from the *Panem et circensis* of the Roman to *Our daily bread* of the Lord's Prayer. Even in nursery rhymes it holds its sway, from the Cocklety Bread (No. 128) of Yorkshire, to the *Pan, pan, pido pan* of the Porteño of Buenos Ayres, which last is our *Puss, puss come to my corner.* In the schools of Spain the frolicsome boys begin a quiet tattoo with their feet, which, if not checked, developes into a regular Horatian *pulsanda tellus,* and this is called Hacer pan Frances—making French bread. And at Cassano d'Adda (Lombardy) I have heard a little lady mutter grace before dinner in this fashion:

> Paternoster
> Cott in del forno,
> Coll moll in dell mezz
> E el crust intorno.

Explaining itself, this requires no translation.

---

* My avuncular relation of the triple spheres.

(214.) SHOW-LADIES. Oh the show-ladies of my youthful days! the glorious glamour of the Thespian throng, the banging of the big drum, the braying of the trumpet, the tumbling of the Tom-fool, the scowling of the villain on the stage at Richardson's show, the halo of the tinsel sheen and the beauteous bangles on the skirt of the heroine's rainbow fairy form! These will linger in my memory till all life's shadows fade away upon the beam of endless day. Oh, the penny duck, the brandy-snap, the parkin in Vicar's Croft, the wild Indian brandishing his calumet (no, that's wrong), his wigwam (no, that's worse—I have it), his tomahawk; the spotted man, the pig-faced lady, the crowd of country bumpkins gazing in awe-struck wonder. And the roaring of the lions, walk up, just agoing to begin, the growling of the bears, only sixpence each, the shrieking of the parrots, positively the last time, all at Wombwell's. Why, when I was a chorister-boy at Leeds, did not our revered old vicar, Walter Farquhar Hook* and his family, our organist, Samuel Sebastian Wesley,† and his pupil, William Spark, all patronise the wild beasts' show? Gone for ever. Would I live my life over again? No. In a certain way the past is delightful; but, I think I've had enough of it. Brock's illumined pyrotechnic display, at the Crystal Palace, when over is only—fireworks. Life is only a dream, and when we awake in another world we shall find that we have only been asleep in this. Oh, for the show-ladies.

CONTRIBUTED BY MR. SAM BLACKBURN, PHŒNIX MILL, BRIGHOUSE.

(215.) FUSSACK, a donkey; in Cockney a *moke*.

(216.) FIRE-POINT, a poker.

(217.) GAITARDS, going a portion of the way with a friend: "I went gaitards with him."

(218.) GAUMLESS, silly or vacant in manner; in Milan, *cilap*; in Spanish, *bobo*.

* The preacher of the boldest sermon, Gen. xlix., 9 (*Guelph*).
† The composer of the noblest anthem "The Wilderness."

(219.) GREASE-HORN, a horn formerly carried on carts to grease the wheels; also used as a term of contempt towards a fawning, insinuating person. In slang, *toady;* old English, *lickspittle;* in Greek, *sycophantos;* in Cockney, *carny.*

(220.) HUGGAN, a hip bone.

(221.) ILL THRIVEN, selfish, narrow-minded.

(222.) MARROW-TO-BONNY, like another in character or conduct, one's double, my alter-ego, a kind of Hulbert and his Wilfrid Murray.

(223.) MENSEFUL, respectable, clean.

(224.) PIGGIN, a lading can; and *pigaud* in Languedoc is a can of wine.

(225.) SLOTCH, a drunkard; in Spanish, *borracho.*

> Antes quando tenia plata
> Mi llamaba don Tomas :
> Y ahora que no tengo
> Es mangia caño, y no mas.—*Argentine Song.*

(226.) STAIL, a handle.

(227.) THORBLE, a wooden spoon used in making porridge.

(228.) TEWS, works hard.

(229.) TASTRIL, a scamp. *Fripon* (French), *pillo* (Spanish dialect).

(230.) THOIL. "He cannot *thoil* to see anyone prosper but himself."

(231.) WHEW'D, whirled round.

(232.) WASTRIL, one who wastes.

(233.) WISHIN, a cushion.

(234.) MERRILS, a game, is also called "Double-study," to distinguish it from "Single-study," one of a simpler kind. It used to be called "Noughts and Crosses," and I have seen it played by the alumni of Montevideo under the name of "Guarismos y Croces." It is a kind of improvised *Solitaire* in principle. Shakespeare alludes to the game in *Mid-*

H

summer Night's Dream, under the name of "Nine men's morris." Of course the *morris* first meant a dance, "Morris-dancers" *(i.e.,* Moorish dancers), and then, any game whatever.

(235.) UNKID.

One of my men, who hails from Warwickshire, occasionally uses the word "unkid" to express the feeling of sadness and regret at the absence of a friend. Speaking of a little child, whose playmate had been absent for a time, he said, "Yes, she is very 'unkid' about her little friend." This expressive word I find used by Blackmore in his beautiful story *Lorna Doone.* The word "unkid," to my mind, very forcibly represents a very expressive word in the Portuguese language, "saudade," which means a tender, loving remembrance of a dear friend, or of a cherished locality. "Tell my dear friend that I have not forgotten where he lives, that I often have 'saudades' of our many happy meetings."—*Leeds Mercury.*

The Spanish *recuerdo* has nearly the same tender meaning; and in a certain sense so has the English pine, not the Yorkshire pine (No. 65). Milton has

> Abashed the devil stood—
> Virtue in her own shape how lovely, saw,
> And *pined* his loss.

In a more forcible way is the Portuguese word *saudade*, which signifies an affectionate, longing, regret for a lost or absent object, much beloved. This word is said to be peculiar to the Portuguese tongue, and to have no verbal equivalent in any other European speech. Leal Conselheiro has: " E porem me parece este nome, tam proprio que o latym, nem otra linguagem que en saiba, nom he pera tal sentido semelhante " (Paris, 1842). I said *verbal,* because, as the sentiment is common to humanity, all civilized languages must have the corresponding expression, whether as a monosyllable or a periphrase. Let us see :

> Thou min'st me o' departed days, departed never to return.—*Burns.*
>
> O Life in Death, the days that are no more.—*Tennyson.*
>
> Still youth remembers with a sigh the days that are no more.
> —*Southey.*

See also Genesis xliii, 30. There is *Lear's* Fool *pining* for the absence of Cordelia *(Shakespeare).*

> Sublatam ex oculis *quærimus* invidi.—*Hor. Carm.*, iii, 24.

Here Horace means by quærimus regret, miss, long for, yearn : this word is in common use in the classics. Now it appears that this Portuguese *saudade* or *sœdade* (an older form) has its representative in the Icelandic *Saknadr*, the Swedish *Saknad* and the Danish *Savn*, both in the general meaning and the special. One must not be induced to think that there is here derivational relationship, or link of origination, unless all belong to some Gothic radical now lost to us. It is a remarkable coincidence of consonantal similarity and identity of meaning : that is all.

(236.) CROFT (Anglo-Saxon), meaning a field or meadow near a house. Though a dictionary word, it is of exclusively Yorkshire use. In Leeds there are Vicar's Croft and King Charles' Croft ; there is Croft, near Darlington ; and the seat of that genial gentleman, Arthur Wilson, Esq., is Tranby Croft. This word is like *ing*, both being Anglo-Saxon, and having the same signification. Information is invited.

(237.) WAYZGOOSE. Clement Blackburn sent me this from the *Brighouse Echo*, 1891 :—

Last Monday afternoon, through the kindness of a few gentlemen doing business with the *Echo*, the staff employed thereon had a very enjoyable excursion. A comfortable waggonette, to which were attached a couple of horses, was in readiness at Park Street at half-past one, and a few minutes later the party took their seats in the anticipation of enjoying a pleasant drive. The weather during the morning had been somewhat threatening, but as we sped along Elland Road we were greeted with the beams of " Old Sol," and his welcome rays generally raised our spirits. Not that our spirits had drooped, oh no ; for one of the P.D.'s had distinctly said in the morning that the " Sun would shine on the *righteous*." By that he meant that we should only be *right* if we took him with *us ;* and thinking it best to believe it rather than prove it, we took the youth along with us.

The word " wayzgoose " is a stranger to me ; like the little boy at a dame's school trying to remember the name of one particular letter of the alphabet : " Aa knaw the beggar bi seet, bud Aa'm noan o' speykin' terms wi him." Is it akin to the London Bean-feast, when members of a firm go off in vans for the yearly outing ? Mr. Hartley, editor of the *Brighouse Echo*, writes that this word is not a Yorkshire word at all, but simply a compositors' and printers' term for an annual outing. I insert it in my book because, if it is not Yorkshire, it ought to be.

(238.) POMFRET CAKES are little round cakes of black Spanish liquorice juice, about the size of a halfpenny, and stamped with a castle *in exergue*, as medallists would say. Pomfret is Yorkshire for Pontefract, and the castle represents Pontefract Castle, where the weak King Richard II. was murdered by order (or connivance) of Bolingbroke, Henry IV. This liquorice root was originally imported from Spain, where it was named *uruzu negro ;* it is now cultivated largely about Protefract. The root is also sold as a stick, and boys love to munch it for its sweet juice. In Uruguay the boys call it *uruzu de palo.* I notice that at the Folk-lore Congress cakes, from all parts of the world were mentioned by the chairman, Mr. Andrew Lang, but strange to say our little black favourite was omitted. Liquorice is one of those English words with two spellings : liquorice and licorice. The former gives a wrong idea that it is connected with liquor, because of the juice ; the latter is the better spelling, as it is nearer to its Greek original, *Glycorrhyza* (sweet-root), as is seen in German *das Süssholz* (sweet-tree). In the Italian *liquirizia* and *regolizia* the first is like our word, and the last like the French *la réglisse*, though how the *r* crept in is a mystery.

(239.) PIKED, an expressive West-Riding word much used in the neighbourhood of Bradford, Halifax, Brighouse, &c. "I *piked* off as quiet as I could ;" meaning "I took myself away": a kind of Yankee skedaddle.

(240.) CHECKS, a game played on the street pavement by little girls, with four pot cubes about an inch in size, and a big porcelain bouncing taw. Sometimes the pieces are made three-cornered, in such a way that however thrown they will stand, like the three legs of the Arms of the Isle of Man (funny ! legs of the Arms). In London it is called *Gob-stones*, and the taw is the *Buck*, but the stones are five, and are anything that can be found in the street : stones, coal, or broken pot. In the college at Montevideo my boys played a similar game with peach stones *(carozo del durazno)*, but these they catch on the back of the hand : first one, then two, three, then four. The ancient game played by the Roman street boy was termed *astragalagantes;* the *astragal* is a knuckle-bone.

REMINISCENCY.

In my younger days Leeds was much smaller, much dirtier than it is now; and the line of the busy throng extended from the Briggate end of Kirkgate to Timble Brig; or, on Sunday evenings, up Lower Head Row, past "Queen Anne," and into Upper Head Row, where the crowd melted away in different directions. On market days Briggate had its stalls on both sides of the street; and amongst the vendors was always to be seen old Mrs. Gibson (a celebrity of my time) selling her yarns in hanks, darning worsted, crewel of divers colours, and threads on bobbins. Leeds was at that time the centre of the Flax-trade; and the many mills of Ives and Atkinson, Marshall, Tatham and Walker, Benyon, and others gave a good notion of buzzing business and honest industry, while their thousands of hands pouring out at meal times enlivened the streets. Where has it all gone? To Prussia, Flanders, Belfast, and other places.

Peter Fairbairn,* in the Kirkstall Road, was the great flax machinery maker. The firm Fairbairn, Greenwood and Batley, called themselves *machinists;* but since the sewing machine makers have appropriated the designation, our firm was obliged to alter their appellation; just as it was with the Music Hall in Albion Street, for since the opening of modern music halls (stages for vane Vances and low Leybournes) the name at *Leeds* mis*leads.*

After our return from Guebwiller, in Alsace, where my

---

* Sir Peter is dead, and the baronetcy has gone to his son, Sir Andrew.

father, brother and sisters taught flax spinning at the factory of Burghardt and Schlumbergér, and where we heard at a concert Mesdames Stockhausen and Bilstein, and Sigismond Neukomm,† Peter Fairbairn sent my father to Bourton, in Somersetshire, to introduce flax machinery. The mill-owner was a Mr. Oliver Maggs, and the place is now called Flax Bourton, where most of the inhabitants were either Sparrows, Farthings, or Maggs, reminding one of the Saviour's question, "Are not two sparrows sold for a farthing?" These people were the most diabolical in character, united to the most sanctified names, for all were either Jeremiah, Habbakkuk, Kezia, Daniel, &c. The firm also sent my brother to Cassano d'Adda, Lombardy; and a Leeds man, John Dyer, was really the first Englishman who introduced this industry to the paesani and contadini: from heckling to carding, from roving to spinning. The card-filleting was supplied by Abraham Goodall, of Brighouse. This Mr. Goodall was the gentleman who got me the situation at Dr. Lundy's Academy, at Brighouse, where, amongst many pupils, I call to mind Clement Blackburn, James Sugden, Teddy Field, Rhodes, Beaumont (of Elland), &c. A colleague of mine was J. I. Berry, now accountant for the Great India Peninsula Railway (a born mathematician), who has published a splendid work on the financial calculations of the varying rupee.

Dr. Lundy, the proprietor of the school, was a very good master, a fine preacher, an amiable man—but rather sensitive. Unfortunately he had a title from a German University (Giessen, I think) which was a cause of much *latent* ridicule; nobody would have displayed such unwisdom as to hint openly. In an evil hour a letter appeared in the local paper signed by Dr. Lundy. In the next paper there was a fierce anonymous attack, and I was supposed to have been the author, as it observed amongst other matter that neither Dr. Hook of Leeds nor Dr. Wesley would have signed their names with their titles, and incidentally adding that if *Mr.* Lundy preferred

† He wrote the music to Barry Cornwall's popular *The Sea ! The Sea !*

such things he could use all the letters of the alphabet. Alas! I had come from Leeds, had been a chorister boy under Dr. Wesley, and listened to the preaching of Dr. Hook. It turned out afterwards that the writer was Fairless Barber, a solicitor. However, there was no displosion, no bitter upbraiding; but I knew it rankled in his mind. He's dead now. R.I.P.

Another instance : My brother-in-law, William Young, came to dine with us, and calamitously addressed the doctor across the table as Mr. Lundy ; and all the boys present, too ! Oh, mountains, fall upon us ! rocks, hide us ! Who could have given the hint? Why, Dyer, of course. Mr. Robert Harley, F.R.A.S., was the Congregational minister at Rastrick — a brilliant preacher, a fine chess player, and a learned mathematician, who had written an abstruse pamphlet on *Cyclical Functions.* The bicycle was not then invented, or some cyclist might have thought the work referrible. George Blackburn, a dear friend of mine (now dead), was a genial man, a good violinist, a connoisseur in painting, music and book-lore. He never missed coming to London if a favourite opera was out, such as *Zampa* or *Masaniello.* Verdi he could not bear. He used to say : " Honey is sweet, but you can't make a meal of it." On one occasion he and I went to see the excavation of a Roman villa near Fixby ; and though knowing him well, I was astonished at the lucid explanation of baths, hot and tepid, atrium, fosse, &c., from a cotton spinner. If ever I was inclined to break the Tenth Commandment it was when I played (strummed ?) on his violin. A mechanical genius of Brighouse was George Goodall (now dead). On one occasion he showed me an electro-moto-machine of his own make and invention, that would have done credit to Faraday. Indeed, all the family of the Goodalls were clever. Mrs. Sunderland was also at Brighouse in my time. To my thinking she was a Jenny Lind and a Patti rolled into one—*Pâte-de-foie-gras.*

When the Polish family (father, mother and son) came to Brighouse to give a concert, and bringing with them their name—Smitanovski (strongly suspected of being in plain English Smith)—they called on us, and in the course of conversation the lady, in good English (or bad Polish*), declared that her musical abilities were so wondrous that she could put a "second to anything." We tried over the *Old Hundredth*, and she in a mezzo-soprano kept continuously a third below; as the tune ends on the tonic, and she finished on a minor third below, this somewhat interfered with the effect of the full close. At the concert, Mrs. Sunderland being present, the son sang in three sharps, whilst his harp twanged in four flats, but as there was only the difference of a semitone, that did not affect the *Simple Muleteer*, especially as he was *not too particular to rules*. It was like the militiaman to his mate: " Tom, you bain't in step." " Ain't I, Bob? Then change yourn." The "Yorkshire Queen of Song" laughed, not loud, but long, and the cachinnation being catching, we all smiled ; but the Smitanovskis, masters of the situation, burst into full trio *Der Spinner und Flachs*.

About the year 1840 I was brought over from Lissieux, in Normandy, and taken to the Parish Church on the Sunday evening. A new light dawned on my mind. I saw the white-robed boys, I heard the silvery voices, the rolling of the organ reverberating round the sacred pile, the deep buzz of intonation in the gallery: all swayed my soul with emotions never felt before. On coming out after service I expressed a wish to become a chorister ; and this desire was soon realised. John Collingwood was the schoolmaster, and being a Londoner, was generally called by the brothers (who were big, bad, boys) " London Duck," only they pronounced it " Loondoon Dook," until the master catching one of them, who was about twenty years old, almost squeezed the life out of him, and entirely deleted the nickname. After that there was peace in the land. By him I was taken to the choirmaster, a Mr. Hill, an alto singer, from Dublin, who scribbled me out a bit of music, which I read at sight. This Hill possessed a flute-like voice. He taught his own classes on the Wilhelm

---

* A little more *polish* and it would have been all right.

system, introduced by John Hullah. I mind that he was the composer of a Christmas duet for boys, which was simplicity itself, melodious and catching that it became a favourite with everybody : *Hail, Christmas, Hail!* Amongst the chorister boys when I was admitted were Hill, the nephew of the choirmaster; the two Deans ; Clarke, afterwards sent to teach at the Deaf and Dumb School, in Dublin ; Ben Clapham ; the two Cravens ; John Jabez Poole, a youth remarkable for his overstrung nervosity ; Whaley Frewer, who, joining the Walker filibustering expedition to Nicuragua, died of the swamp fever ; Ogden Dayson and his brother, &c. As for Archibald Ramsden, he came after I left, when my voice broke. I heard afterwards, in a kind of stage aside, that the new choristers were mighty superior to us ; adding, in sartorial saw, *that we were not a patch on 'em.* Of course we *seniores priores* could not admit that : but going one Sunday evening, I heard Archibald Ramsden, and his voice soared heavenward in thrilling tones that in my excited mind I thought would not have misbecome the hierarchy of heaven, accompanied by their golden harps. My heart felt a pang, but not from envy. The men were Jakeman ; Wood, afterwards transferred to Carlisle Cathedral ; Cawthra, a public singer in the oratorios and concerts, possessing a splendid tenor ; Michael Clapham, an alto ; Rider, the parish clerk ; Carville, a whipmaker ; Williamson, who owned a bass so clear and profound that he was the only one (so it was said) who could dive down deep to E the first ledger-line below the lines* in Wesley's heavenly anthem. There were several gentlemen amateurs, two being Mr. Smith (of Headingley) and Mr. Tom Tennant (of Woodhouse). When Mr. Smith was married, he required all the quire to go down to his place for the purpose of singing at the ceremony ; and after that we were sent to the Royal Oak to *restore* ourselves, as the French term it. Each boy had 5s., buns and gingerbeer ; each man had——what he liked, and no doubt liked what he had. The mirth was kept up till after 9 p.m., and an incident took place which was indelibly

---

* Bass clef, of course.

impressed on my mind. It appears that a few glasses and tumblers got broken, and someone proposed that the pieces should be carefully collected and privately pushed under the grate, when none would be the wiser; at least until we were far away. There was universal acquiescence. Universal? No. Cawthra quietly remarked, looking at the broken glasses: "Why I think the lot won't come to 2s., so that's only 2d. a-piece, which is cheap for our good name. Just fancy the landlord saying: 'Why them beggarly chaps thro' t' Parish Church hes gone away and stuck some brokken glass up t' chimley.'" Need I say, the landlord was called in, the *débris* shown, damages enquired about. Mark what the host said: "Them! Oh, that's nowt. I san't tak nowt for 'em. It's an accident. Good neet all." Cawthra was right. I met this singer, the man of rectitude, twenty years after in Burmantofts. He was walking feebly; and from what he said, as he was too old to sing, he was living on a pension allowed him for past services.

It has been said that noise is music in the wrong key. In the case of Thomson he had a magnificent voice, so he said. This, as he disdained to cultivate it, he kept as a thing to be admired by his friends and owned by himself, like a collector of old fiddles, who cannot play himself. He owned to me that a great organist had told him that he possessed a voice that would be a fortune to him if properly cultivated, and that had he, the great organist, been the fortunate owner of it he would now be riding in his carriage. But what is voice without cultivation? A costermonger bawling out his cabbages in the street may have a fine voice, but he would hardly be engaged at the opera. Thomson had a loud voice, and as he lived next door to me I had the full benefit of it. If I had then known what a recent philosopher tells, I should have been blest with less singing in my ears and he, less singing in his voice. But listen: One very serious fault the ass has: he does not possess a musical voice. But he evidently thinks he has: just like Thomson. Moreover, it is a powerful voice, and strikes upon the aggrieved human ear in a way that is painful. But by a wonderful arrangement the donkey brays not unless he can simultaneously raise aloft his tail. A simple means of keeping his vocal powers in check is to suspend a brick from his tail. A useful hint to suffering man. Why did not nature extend this beneficent arrangement to the braying variety of mankind? If these had been gifted with a caudal appendage, as Lord Monboddo supposed some men have been, but subsequently worn off by sitting, and if nature had made it a condition of human braying that the said appendage should be raised aloft, how many gifted persons might, to the advantage of the public ear, have been forbidden to appear abroad without a brick dangling behind them!

There is another enemy of man's repose—to wit, the untimely-crowing cock. As the donkey cannot bray unless he raises his tail, so the cock cannot crow without elevating his head. A spar placed over the one on which he roosts, at such a height as to prevent him from raising his head, is an effectual silencer: like the mute on the bridge of a fiddle. We refer to these ingenious devices partly on account of their intrinsic value to suffering humanity, and partly as evidencing practical philanthropy. Another is the man who says: "You know I can't read a note of music, sing entirely by ear; but my ear is simply perfect." Such a man singing in the quire was Bream (this was not his name), and he usually learnt his part, when he did learn it at all, by listening to his next door neighbour, whose services he often requited by criticising his performance with the addition of a supercilious query as to its correctness. When the neighbour combined vocal ability with a warm temper, trouble was apt to follow. It was torture to hear him sing after Tallis' "O Lord, open thou our lips," " An' ou' mou' sha' shew fo' thy prai," a broken, lisping monophone where the final consonants were eliminated, as they say in algebra. After all, the Psalmist advises us to seek peace and ensue it.

Deliver me from the man who brags of having an ear, who tells everybody that his ear is perfect, and that it causes him exquisite agony to hear one sing false. Perhaps even a great musician may hear false notes without feeling exquisite agony, or even further thrilling sensation through his being, than a tendency to eloquent profanity.

At the Parish Church at Leeds, though there were four daily services, our duties were only in the evening and twice on Sunday, for which we boys received four pounds a year and the leaders (Decani and Cantoris) five pounds, as being primus inter pares. Besides, we boys attended every morning for practice in the vestry from eight till nine, and received a penny a time, if present; which payment was made every Saturday morning, so that with our coppers we were " passing rich." An old man, lanky and lean, used to wait at a side gate with cakes and sweets to sell. O the delicious cakes, O the dulcet sweets! Years after, on finding myself at Leeds, I went to the old locality wondering if the man was still alive. Why, there he is, the identical pie-man, not a bit older! When no one was looking, I bought one and retired with my prize. Pah! Is that the cake that——? I gave it to a small boy, who, no doubt, thought the man a fool for giving away such a savoury cake. But boys will eat anything. There was young Van Cortlandt at Richmond, who was passionately fond of a h'pny red-herring, even after a good dinner. But the spine-bone of that herring—this he would grill over the gas in the class-room and eat with relish, all smoky as it was.

When the choristers stayed to partake of the Holy Communion, some of the congregation invaded our stalls, amongst them, on one occasion, was a Mr. Maude, from Knowsthorpe Hall, who, it was whispered, was perpetual church-warden—whether he was re-elected by the vestry out of deference to the vicar, or from his imposing appearance, I cannot say—tall, grand, with a sour and angry mien, but, bless you, that scowling look was not in conformity with the geniality of his heart, nor the mildness of his manner. The ruffled surface-water, wind-tossed above, below the quiet still of the profound deep—as you will see. He sat on one occasion next to me : now I had in my pocket a penny (copper, in those days) and a sixpence. To contribute to the oblations, sixpence was too much, a penny was too little. Could I ask the great man to change me sixpence. Absurd ! gentlemen of his position have no such possession as thrip'ny-bits. The matter was pressing. The collector was advancing. My face was burning with shame.

I whispered in his ear ; he had to lean over me to hear.
His scowl disappeared, like a lowering cloud clearing away,
a beauteous beam of a smile stole athwart his countenance.
He took my sixpence and gave me two thrip'ny bits.

At Christmas we all dined, men and boys, at the vicarage :
grand for us boys. Plum-pudding, roast-beef, and the games
of hunting for sixpences in hillocks of flour, turned out of
a basin ; or bobbing for apples dangling from a string ; after
that, presents of knives and books from young Hook and
the little Misses Hook. Of course the dinner was preceded
by the usual Non nobis Domine. Before breaking up we
had rounds, glees, songs and madrigals, "Old Thomas Day,"
"Great Tom is cast," "Would you know my Celia's
charms," "Our Sophia (House a' fire)," &c., &c. For
several nights about X'mastide we trudged to the suburban
seats to sing outside the mansions of the gentry who
frequented the Parish Church, for which we reaped a rich
harvest. On one occasion I received as my share fifteen
shillings—a tidy sum when the funds were divided amongst
several men and ten boys or so.

A young lady made each of us boys a present of half-a-
dozen frilled collars of the finest linen, which we had to wear
out of doors as well as in the choir. This we did not very
much like, as the street-boys called them dog-collars : bear
in mind that the verger was named dog-nauper (No. 111).
In my singing days, Silhouettes began to be in the fashion.
They were portraits cleverly cut out of black paper, certain
parts touched up in gold, and the whole pasted on a neat
cardboard. Well, ours were done by a professor, and all
expenses paid by a gentleman (Mr. Brooks), who took a
fancy for us. These Silhouettes, it appears, were named
after a Mons. Shilouette, a minister of Louis XVI., who in
a time of political extravagance advocated economy in
finance, dress and comestibles. Even in portraits he led
the way by having his taken as a——silhouette. This Mr.
Brooks was a young medical student who had a strong
liking (II Samuel i, 26) for us chorister-boys. He took us
out for walks, gave us books ; Dayson a musical box and
me Keble's " Christian Year," in particular. On one
occasion he led about a dozen of us to a pie-shop and gave

us so much to eat—pie, tart, cake and ginger beer, parkin, brandy-snap and lemonade—that it must have cost a couple of pounds.

At the back of the Church was a dreary place where we boys used to wait for the morning practices, and if no teaching-master came we had all kinds of games over the tombstones, round the graves, &c., until the sexton (a Mr. Pickard) had many a chase on his part, and many a race on ours, but his *pursy*, puffing energy was no match for our *perse*vering rapidity. Do not be shocked at our seeming irreverence. We were only boys, and boys have the power of turning everything into mirth; they are profane* but "rien n'est sacré aux pompeurs." Do you think we had no proper professional pride, no veneration for our cathedral-like church, no enthusiasm for our heavenly music? In the very service, I have known a boy to have an apple under his surplice, and, furtively stooping to remove a score, has given a sly munch; often has one been singing divinely "Take heed unto me" while he has been polishing off a lollipop. The Saviour himself was not everlastingly a "man of sorrows." He, the Redeemer, stooped to make a pun (John i, 42).

The pupils of the organist were Crane, Harding and Spark. Of Crane I may say that the inventive genius of us boys be-nicknamed him Walking Crane, his long legs, his nice nose thereunto agreeing. Of Harding, I can only say that he adapted Byron's "There be none of Beauty's daughters" to an air in B flat major, in which he starts off on the sub-dominant sounding as if a fellow bounced unannounced into your study with a shout "Well! here I am." The sudden sub-dominant sound to the *ear* gave the impression to its cousin, the *eye*, a note of interrogation (?) which note always looked as if it were a man jumping from the ground in amazement. On recalling my music memories I find that Dr. Horsley does the same in his "See the Chariot," only in his case he begins on the sub-tonic as an ascending leading note to the tonic, while Harding's sub-dominant fell. Consequently they may be right and I

---

* Fanum, a sacred place.—See?

wrong, but experientia *docet*, yes experience *does it*.

Regarding William Spark, I must acknowledge that there was a wonderful amount of respect for him : Dr. Wesley always treated him differently from the others. His musical abilities, even then beginning to develop, his gentlemanly carriage, his winning ways to us boys (boys are discerning) all marked the man ; and at private rehearsals we were accustomed to join with a will in his early piece, a setting of Campbell's "The Spirit of Britannia," where the martial music echoes invocative words, and the words sympathise with the tune. Since that retrospective time I have been in various parts of the New and Old World and now I am again in England, I find that he has amply ful-filled his early promise ; the mantle of the great master has fallen on him. As a literary man his style is gossipy and attractive, and his "Musical Memories" are an everlasting testimony of his writing powers and the noble admission to see merit in others.

Walter Farquhar Hook was one of the first churchmen of the day, very prominent in the Tractarian controversies of the times. He took a leading part on the side of Newman, now a cardinal of the Catholic Church. No. 90 Tract caused as much ferment in the ecclesiastical world as did John Wilke's famous No. 45 in the politics of a former epoch. As a preacher he possessed a persuasive elegance well suited to warm the imagination of the mind and move the passions of the soul. As an author he was an historian of credit and merit. He wrote an Ecclesiastical Dictionary and "Lives of the Archbishops of Canterbury*; these ought to have been amply sufficient to have made him a bishop, but, though a Chaplain in Ordinary to Her Majesty, it was said that one sermon (already hinted at in this book) offended the Royal Lady of Windsor. Mr. Glad-stone, however, says preferment was frequently offered to him after he became Dean of Chichester ; but I wonder why such was not offered before. His son-in-law, the Rev. W. R. W. Stephens, observes that it was too late for him

---

* Wish he had lived long enough to have included himself in his "Lives."

to take episcopal duties, but he was offered higher deaneries.
This may have been relational partiality. A fluent orator,
a sound Anglican, a clear writer, a positional man, he was
far fitter for a see than was a Charles Thomas Longley, of
Ripon, afterwards of Canterbury, who rose————————
The Vicar's pet idea was to form districts in the sur-
roundings of Leeds, and he erected about twenty
additional churches. He had the winning facility of
gathering round him the respectable serious youth of the
town, Edward Jackson, the most amiable of men, now
a Reverend Canon, and for many years superintendent
in St. James' Sunday School, where I was a scholar ; Alfred
Brogden Butterworth, who went to St. John's College,
Cambridge (my protector and guide), and who died of con-
sumption at Shipley ; Richard Twigg, subsequently clergyman at Wednesbury ; Samuel Kettlewell, Booker, and
others. The Vicar, whose spirit was finely touched to find
issues, as Shakespeare has it, had one little failing. But the
greatest of minds, minds the smallest of foibles. Even the
power-possessing preacher *Hook* had an *Eye* on one who
came to Leeds, one who poured forth a *flood* of eloquence.
Now Flood was Irish, and the Irish are by nature gifted
with a *torrent* of speech, and our Vicar went to hear him.
Was this invidious ? No. Inquisitive ? Perhaps so. But
did not the greatest statemen, the most brilliant orators, the
deepest thinkers, the finest writers, all go surreptiously to
hear the gift-of-tongues—Irving ? It is human, so let us be
humane. A second something similar, related to an Alfred
Barry, now a bishop. But Dr. Hook wants not my elogy ;
my panegyric will not bestow on him a merit, which he
had not before. The last time I saw my loved old Vicar
was at Chichester, when I was working at Westhampnet.
He was dean, still in harness but feeble with years, and I
remembered the former genial man, stability in manners
and ability in intellect.

At Leeds I gained the Lord Wharton Bible (Bible,
Common Prayer, new and old metrical version of the Psalms,
all bound in one) for repeating by heart the seven penitential Psalms, the Church Catechism and the Beatitudes.
This I wrapped in cloth and carefully put away, using an

older one. Next year we scholars were told to bring our bibles. On uncovering mine, it was so clean that the superintendent told me : "You can't have read yours much ; I must therefore give the prize (half-a-sovereign) to Joseph Imeson." This gentleman was George Hills, now Bishop of British Columbia. When I got home I cried bitterly. Joe Imeson's book was dirty and dog-eared, and in my childish way I thought he must have used it as a football. I remember that at the Sunday School, this reverened gentle-man once indulged in a *leetle* fun, Asking me : "Who were the Israelites ? " I answered "The Childrern of Israel." Of another he asked : " And who were the Jacob-ites ? " The reply was " The Children of Jacob." So have I heard H.M.I. of Schools, the Rev. Mr. Mitchell, ask at an examination " What reason have we for supposing that Robinson Crusoe's Isle was not uninhabited ? " Dead silence. This was his own reply: " Because when he arrived he saw a little *cove*, and a *swell* on the water." When about seven years old, I was taken to the Philosophical Hall, and I remember seeing a piece of leather made from the tanned skin of 'Mary Bateman, the Yorkshire Witch, who was hanged at York Castle in 1809. She it was who prophesied that an egg should be laid, on which would be written Christ's coming—this really occurred. The ignorant believed it to be super-natural, but it was natural enough, and cruel too.

Politics in my time ran high. We had no Conservatives nor Liberals, no Home-rulers nor Unionists, only Blues and Yellows, Tories and Whigs. We had also a supposed dangerous class, called Radicals (Green), who wanted to root (radix) up abuses and make reforms. Some of their tenets have since become law. The Borough that erst had returned a Macaulay had recourse to James Garth Marshall,* from a brilliant writer to a mediocre flax-spinner : such a dearth of political ability that we were obliged to borrow from Birmingham a Quaker corn merchant. On the hust-ings at Woodhouse Moor Joseph Sturge declares that it is time for the people to educate the Government, which was thought *a lapsus linguæ;* and his remark that the national

---

* Never trust a double-barrelled name.

I

education proposal was not na——tional, was supposed to be another slip, until after a 'dead pause, the point was appreciated and a thundering roar from the hearers shewed they were in touch with the speaker. After the speech we took his horses out of the carriage and made ourselves beasts of traction, and along with a shout and a roar and din we perambulated the streets; then a boy, John Cooper Malcom,* fell on the spikes of the railings on which he was standing; then Joseph Sturge lost the election, and I lost—my silk handkerchief. In the Mixed Cloth Hall the Vicar spoke to an expectant crowd—observing that he wished every working man's child to be as well educated as his own daughters—a roar of disapprobation—and he retired in a huff, to be succeeded by a mealy-mouthed man, who perorated : " Why are we building jails there (Armley)? why barracks there (Newtown)?"—mob yelling him down. A third speaker in a mystified manner observed that the proposed Education Bill was like opening the door inside out, at which the people laughed, knowing well that he meant the door opened outward when it ought to have opened inward. " You will all be sent," continued the orator demagogue, " to a reformatory, like Luther and Melancthon, if you don't look out." Someone cried out " Wha, Aa thought them chaps wor Reformers !" " Re formers !" cried the spouter, with withering scorn, " why you ———— ; look here, my fellow men "——interruption from the playful mob, by some shouting : " Fellow indeed why thaa's t' fellow and we's t' men." Mobs are half monkey and half tiger. Oh, we were a model town, what with plumpers, split votes, and what not. The lodge franchise was yet unborn, but it was inchoate. D'Israel was not known. The man who had a vote to sell, sold it— not openly. " If," contended he, " a singer has a voice he sells it, a dancer sells her legs, a preacher his gospel, pugilist his fist, and if," said the publican, " I can't sell two pots of beer where I sold one before, of what use is 'suff'rings' to me ?"——only he did not mean that; but it was near enough : the suffrage to some is a suffering, i

---

* Now Borough Coroner and Solicitor.

judged by their callousness to their voting power, and their caligation to future effects. "Yes," continued Boniface, "if I am a publican I'm not a sinner. A man had better foul his body with beer than file his mind with meanness : them's my sentiments !" Better thinkers held that Tory, Whig and Radical did not become clearer to a man's mind by definition ; but the words themselves gathered by iteration a strangely strong stamp of honour, or plausibility, or infamy. The Tory was a high-souled gentleman, or was supposed to be ; the Whig a man who would make many changes ; but the Radical was a bad fellow who would root up all institutions ordained by God and established by law. The Tory sneered about the *cant* of Reform, and those who had seceded from Reform to slide back to Toryism were greeted with the epithet of the *recant* of Reform.

These were the days of Mechanics' Institutes and Birkbeck Societies. Lord Brougham's "schoolmaster was abroad ;" where the phrase is often now misunderstood, as intending crass ignorance, whereas *he* signified that education was beginning to spread. Then we had no electric telegraph, no Pullman's car,* no tramways,† no Davenport Brothers, no Theosophy. Our third class carriages of railway were open to the sky ; human cattle-trucks, no seats. Leaving Leeds at 6 a m., one arrived at King's Cross at 10 p.m., shunted at little bye-stations to let many other trains pass. Then the postage to Milan was 2s. 4d. for the quarter-ounce, and 8d. to London.

Our music of sentiment was "Meet me by moonlight alone," Haynes Bayly's "She wore a wreath of roses," "We met : 'twas in a crowd," "It was nature's gay day, and bright smiling May day," Moore's "Timid tear," &c. ; or, if we were inclined to be merry, we had "The gay cavalier," "Gaily the troubadour," "In the day's we went a-gipsying," Lover's "Och hone ! widdy Macrae," &c. James Rice, the first imitation of the black, and who had made a fortune by his nigger impersonations, had just left us "Jump Jim Crow," "Sich a gitting up stairs," "Some one in the house wid Dinah," &c. He netted a fortune ;

---

* Good name ! pull man.   † Sir James Ou*tram*.

£1000 a night was paid him at the Adelphi (London) for
his songs, break-downs, walk-round and nigger guffaw : by
a skilful allusion to the topics of the day* he became
very popular, and may be said to have been the
precursor of Henry Russell, the Christie, and Mohawk
Minstrels, and the host of banjo-beaters of this present. As
for instrumental music, we had " March in Lodoiska,"
" Reichstadt Waltz," and Labitsky's " La Pluie de Perles,"
" Les Cloches du Monastère," and the noisy " Battle of
Prague." Young Neesom, with a long body on
interminable legs, a long face and arms without end
(tentum pellis et ossa fuit) was a fine fellow at this warfare
in the Bohemian capital. How his fingers lingered over
the cries of the wounded, how he thumped the cannon
balls here, how he bumped the shells there ; his advancing
cavalry galloped over the keys, the bugles sounded, the
fight was fought, victory followed, and " See the conquering
hero comes," and there————an end. My pianoforte
attainments were limited to " Oh dear, what can the matter
be ;" and they who heard my music sympathised with the
words. The said music I fished out in the treble, while the
base-hand sustained the key-note throughout, as I dared not
wander away for fear of losing it. This unvarying mono-
tonic base detracted from the brilliancy of the execution,
and also gave the effect of a droning bagpipe.† Dr. Johnson
once observed that he knew a man who had but one idea,
and that was a wrong one. I was a boy (only ten) who had
but one tune, and that was a right one. One young lady
complimented me (I thought so at first) by saying that
I played with *feeling*, because I was everlastingly *feeling* for

---

* Years after, I once knew a nigger whose name was———— ;
forget it now. But he was gifted with this typical-topical allusiveness
It was at Hastings. The previous evening Sims Reeves had been
singing at the Rink. Our sable minstrel warbled forth ;

I shall never be happy again,
Till someone believes
I can sing like Sims Reeves,
I shall never be happy again.

† A bag is a sack, a pipe is a butt ; therefore a bagpipe is
sackbut——Q. E. D.

the keys. "Oh dear, what can the matter be?"

The originator of the *Leeds Mercury* had his shop in Briggate, before Queen Anne was removed. Barran (afterwards M.P.) had his clothes-shop over Leeds Bridge, on the left hand side. Richard Oastler, the great reformer, was plunging into the sharebroker mania of '46 ; indeed, everybody was buying and selling shares. King Hudson ruled supreme. Watson, of Albion Street, bought, and the euphoniously-named firm of Park Row—Grimshaw, Kershaw and Bagshaw, or some such style—sold. Old Benny Gott was combing his wool, and acting generously to his workpeople ; to one especially, a young man who lost his right hand in the machinery, and whom Mr. Gott (in his everlasting laud) sent to a night school that he might learn to write with his left, with the intention of putting him into the counting-house. So different to Sh—sh—s, who remarked to his old workman "You are too old to work now, Jemmy." "Yes, maister, Aa'm tew ou'd ta wark now, after fifty years on it." "I thought so," said his master. "As you're of no further use to me you'd better leave, and go into the workhouse."

One of the reporters of the *Leeds Mercury*, a Mr. Davidson, was a very clever man. He wrote a grammar in which he aired a peculiar fad ; that is, instead of the old nomenclature verb, noun, pronoun, &c., he substituted word, name, for-word, shout-word, connecting-word. This would have been right enough if the Anglo-Saxon had been allowed freely to develop instead of being obfuscated by the Norman-French partially eclipsing it ; then we might have evolved such words as we have now, wheelbarrow, railroad, tramcar, &c. For scientific words we must have recourse to Greek and Latin. Otherwise, as in the plastic German, we might have had such terms as :

Earth-writing	Erdschreibung	Geography.
Star-law	Sternkunde	Astronomy.
Counting-knowledge	Rechenkunst	Arithmetic.

As it is, it is better. Besides the mellifluous addition to English, such words as geography are international ; and all nations can understand them as well as we all understand the Arabic cyphers 1, 2, 3, 4, &c.

Old Tommy Fenteman sold his books and fiddles at his old curiosity shop of bric-à-brac; Beckett kept his bank in Albion Street; Knock-'em-down Tommy ranted and sniffled out.

> The gospel ship has long been sailing,
> Bound for Canaan's peaceful shore;

and Alice Man sold her "Peace-egg" and the "Bold Slasher" in the Central Market; and I trudged off to school to learn my "Corduroy Koloky, Ke Ki Kod" (so it sounded to me), and Big Ben, the bellman, bawled " Lost, to-day, a barn, about five year owd, hed on a white brat and——" Two factory lasses meet, one with her mill shawl over her head, the other, out for a holiday, dressed in gaudy colours, a velvet hat surmounted by a flowing feather. "Where's ta bahn, Bet, to-day? Isn't t' at wark?" "Noa," replies the York Street beauty; " I'm bahn t'at Gardens. Bud tell me, Tett Mabbet, does me feather wag?" *This was* in Saxon Lane. Another eccentric was a constable,* with one eyebrow white and the other black. Some of his sayings were remarkably odd. "Luke," said he, "ther's a haystack o' oats." Another time he found a shawl, and when asked if he had *cried* it, answered: " Ay for suer; Aa cried out up t' chimley when nobbody wor abaat." He was not such a fool as he looked, though. This will show : In the course of conversation with a friend, who remarked that " he enjoyed very bad health," our police constable observed : " Why, Daudy, I never heärd o' anybody *enjoying bad* health." A bit of a wag, too, when he said: " When a man's on t' *loose* he's suer to get *tight.*" Again: " How's thee mother, lad?" he asked of a boy. " Wha, sho's get her deäth o' co'ud." " Is sho dëad?" To a man who had grown wonderfully thin he said : " Wha, tha's noan t' same man : tha's like Jack's knife, which had changed its blade and handle mony times."

There was a Mr. Burton who had a music class near the " Ring-a-Bells," and who taught on the movable *Do* system.

---

* Sir Robert Peel's New Police were not then organised; since called after him Peeler and Bobby.

He knew about as much music as a cat does of the chromatic scale. He used to conduct with his walking stick in lieu of a bâton : as for time, he took his own. The practice was not much better than a Dutch concert, in which every singer sings what he likes. One conscientious fellow on my right "missed the start," as he afterwards expressed it, and during the whole of the chorus vainly endeavoured to catch up. But as he chose to introduce the opening bars instead of taking up the strain, his well-meant efforts were productive of nothing but confusion. Another singer, in a battered high hat, and a coat three sizes too small for him, laboured under painful doubts as to his natural voice. He would sing falsetto, tenor, bass and double bass with admirable impartiality, seeking to find which was the best suited for him. At one moment his vocalisation would take the form of a thin squeal, as he strained his neck and started his eye-balls to "fetch that there note." At another, a prodigious roar would issue from his throat, which would entirely disconcert all. Meanwhile the conductor beat time—one, two, and three. I have since heard that he has become a great musician, quantity or quality I do not know. If muddling Mozart, spoiling Spohr, or handling Handel constitute greatness, well, he was a g.m.

The Wesleys were John, the founder of Methodism, and Charles, the poet, author of

> Come let us anew
> Our journey pursue,
> Roll round with the year,
> And never stand still
> Till the Master appear.

Charles, the sweet singer, was also a flute player, and his wife used to sing Handel's oratorio airs. This Charles had two sons, Samuel the musical prodigy, and a Charles, who was a favourite organist of George III. Of Samuel it must be said that he was a master on the organ, and had written a fugue for that instrument so operose that it was supposed no one else could play it.* He had the credit of introducing to the English musical world the works of Sebastian

---

* A friend tells me that that's nothing. He says he can write a piece of music that no mortal man can play. I believe it.

Bach, the great German organ fugue writer ; and to show
his devotion to his idol he named his son after himself and
his friend, Samuel Sebastian Wesley. One of Bach's fugues
was a play on his own name : the H in German is the B
(made natural) of the key of B flat major. From John
Wesley the Methodist to Samuel Wesley the church organist
(dissent reverting to the established religion) is explicable on
remembering that the Dissenters had then no organs. Dr.
S. S. Wesley was born in 1810, and in 1842 was organist
at Leeds Parish Church, but being of a restless disposition
resigned in 1849, passing from cathedral to cathedral in
search of his real ideal of musical amenities. He had
written a tract on cathedral music, in which he argued that
devotion would better be advanced if the congregation did
the listening and the choir the singing. This prince of
church music was an unrivalled pedallist ; perhaps there was
one equal, and that was Felix Bartholdy Mendelssohn.
These two I heard on the grand organ in the Universal
Exhibition of '51. Wesley's Credo has a mass of pedal
work. The finest anthem ever written, " The Wilderness,"
has the true oratorio recitative, and a plaintive piece of
" Sorrow and Sighing," a measured melody of melancholy
music, followed by a rattling chorus, " And the ransomed of
the Lord," quite in the style of Handel. When I was
erecting a galvanised corrugated iron church at Cobham, in
Surrey, the clergyman—the Rev. Wellesley Wesley—told me
that he was the grandson of old Sam Wesley, and that the
family was originally Irish ; that both names were pronounced Wesley, so that some branches retained the *old
spelling* Wellesley, as the Cowleys, the Morningtons, the
Wellingtons : and other branches retained the *old pronunciation* Wesley, and for that reason he was christened with
both names—Wellesley Wesley. Of Ibsen's heredity, the
Wesleys are a confirmation. Sebastian, Old Sam, Charles,
Earl of Mornington* were all musicians, and Wellington's
" Up Guards and at them," at Waterloo, was a military
song, though never set to music. At the Music Hall (not
the meretricious modern, so called) in Albion Street, Dr.

---

* " Here in Cool Grot."

Wesley gave a rehearsal of Haydn's "Seasons." Miss Dolby* was singing "Peep through the hedge and let me know if they can see us two." As this was unaccompanied, so it was the more prominent, an arch look from the doctor set the ladies tittering. On another occasion we were hurrying through the "Messiah," when for some reason or other all the orchestra stopped playing except the first fiddle (a Mr. White), who finished a florid run in such a clear and staccato style that the doctor's face beamed with delight. Nothing pleased him more than perfection in execution; like Handel, he was *uomo indiavolato* if a note was too sharp or too flat; and many a time in the church have I heard a discordant crash on the organ to drown a false note. He was very insistent. A young lady who had "doubled the part," as theatricals say, in the absence of the principal prima, was singing a solo from the "Messiah:" her voice was good enough, but her affectation was so great that she warbled forth "But thou did'st not *live* his *Saul* in *Hull*." The doctor (his brow black as night) said in a voice as raucous as a rasp: "Saul did not live in Hull: go away, and learn English." We were all aghast. At a concert in the Old Cloth Hall (behind Kirkgate) he introduced a new Gregorian style in which the sustaining note was the *third* instead of the *first*, thus:

My—soul doth magnify the—Lord ⎱ S. S. Wesley.
1 2————— 3 ——— — 4 5 ⎰

My soul doth magni—fy the—Lord ⎱ Old Chant.
1 ————— 2 3—— 4 ⎰

This was wonderfully well received. After that we all sang "God Save the Queen," and following "O Father, whose Almighty power," from "Judas Maccabæus," to show (as the doctor maintained) that there was a striking likeness, and consequently, plagiary of tune somewhere. But what of that? There is a strain in Sullivan's "Lost Chord," in Handel's "Dead March in Saul," and in Braham's "Death of Nelson,"† identical. Is not our bacchanalian "We

---

* Afterwards Madame Sainton-Dolby, having married Mons. Sainton, the primo violino.

† Air: fa, mi (re, do), re, si, do.

won't go home till morning," the Frenchman's " Malbrook
s'en va-t-en guerre ?"   " The Death of Nelson " is almost
note for note a " Breton Sailor's Song ;" ay, and the very
sailor who is said to have shot our hero at Trafalgar : and
Mozart's Kyrie Eleison (" Twelfth Mass ") begins like the
music-hall jingo " We don't want to fight."   The music
(temp. Henry VIII.) to the nursery rhyme " Hush a bye,
baby " is the very air* of the Irish Lilibulero in " Tristram
Shandy."   But the wonder is that there is such a variety in
airs, when there are only eight notes to work with.   Similar
is the case that thousands of languages and millions of
words arise from the permutation and combination of about
thirty alphabetic characters.†   Revenons à nos moutons.
At the concert just mentioned we tried a new piece, " In
exitu Israel," a kind of declamatory recitative, which was
heard with enthusiasm.   Dr. Wesley was a great angler, and
I have seen him at Harewood Bridge, opposite the Ship
Inn, following the gentle craft, accompanied by Martin
Cawood.   He was there with his elaborate tackle : rod,
silk, winch and reel ; I was a little way off with mine, a
stick, thread and " crookelt " pin ; and perhaps I had a
better catch than the great man.   I fished above the stream
because, like the wolf and the lamb of fable-lore, I did not
wish to disturb the water to mar his sport.   On one
occasion he broke his leg.

The Histrionic Art was carried out at a dingy theatre
down Hunslet Lane, and that was the only one Leeds
possessed ; in fact Pritchard, who excelled in such plays as

---

* See *Early English Musical Magazine*, January, 1891.

† " Think for a moment," shrewdly observes Mr. Wilson Barrett,
" how limited in number are the human passions ; then remember that
for two thousand five hundred years these passions have been used
thousands of times as the mainspring of dramatic action, and you will
see how difficult originality becomes."

To this I, the present writer, should answer that in these
passions an infinity of moral, psychological, and philosophical
subtleties continually germinate, and offer an inexhaustible stock to the
close observer, who knows how to discover and utilise them.   Indeed,
the passions may be, for dramatic purposes, as few as the strings of a
fiddle ; but what an endless number of tunes and variations will not
the consummate artist evolve.

"Douglas," was the lessee of three theatres—Leeds, York and Hull. Fancy, one company for three towns! After many years a wooden theatre was built in King Charles' Croft, next to a circus kept by Pablo Fanque (real name, Darby), and whose wife was killed by the falling in of some of the scenery. Her funeral was graced with a splendid equipage of property horses. Since then Mr. Hobson has catered for the Leeds theatrical taste, as has, later on, Wilson Barrett, the great actor, who created "Denver" in the "Silver King."* Henry Russell, called with his simple songs of two keys, where the *canto spiegato* always modulated to the key of the dominant. The "Infant Sappho" (afterwards known as Miss Vining, of the Princess' Theatre, London,) electrified us with her mimetic melody. And D'Oyly Carte came to give us burlesque imitations of "The Ship on Fire," "Woodman Spare that Tree," &c., tableau, voice and piano.

As for oil-paintings, there was Rhodes; I have his "Fishing Boy" now, and it is valued at £20. Then there was Robinson, who painted a view of Leeds looking from the high ground beyond "The Bank;" and old Sam Dyer, whose little landscapes, with sheep, are the gems of his surviving family—*sempre pecore*, as Arthur Dyer used to say. My father painted the portrait of a splendid Newfoundland dog which belonged to a Mr. Clapham, who kept a chemist's shop in Briggate, for which portrait he received fifty guineas. This dog was so knowing that he could do anything, so said his owner, except talk and draw a three months' bill—his master could do both.

Of the mutability of words in meaning and form, the word masher† is an instance. Successively toff, dandy, swell;

---

* A witticism of his worth recording is that a friend meeting him, said "I saw old Jayson yesterday, but as he has lost all his teeth he mumbled so that I couldn't understand a word he said—it was all Greek to me." Wilson Barrett replied: "Nonsense. It wasn't Greek: it was *Gum*-Arabic."

† The origin of this word is not known. It came to the fore in 1885. Now the French *mâcheur à vide* means to live on air; and mâcher, to mince or chew, just as the masher does the end of his stick. When can a man choose whether to smoke or chew? When he *chews*.

it was in my youth a Blood.* There was Blood Atkinson,
who dressed to death, like Sally Hatch, as the saying is ; or
tiré à quartre épingles, according to the French. He was
as great a swell as they make them. Familiarly called
Mimmy Atkinson, his soubriquet arose thus : His name
was originally James; this was abbreviated into Jim,
lengthened to Jimmy, diminished to My, and reduplicated
to Mimmy. Mease, who formerly had a flax mill at
Stokesley, was another Blood.

Old Morgan, grocer, pawnbroker, householder, and parish
road surveyor at the Bank (a Leeds slum), the owner of
Morgan's Yard, had a little chapel in Spring Street, which
held about twenty-five persons (the chapel, not the street).
He used to wear an old brown coat, all buttoned up before ;
and he preached somewhat like Simon Kilham (of the sect
of the Kilhamites), a doctrine that was most assuredly an
anticipation of the Theosophy of Madame Blavatsky and
her brilliant follower, Annie Besant, who modulated from
Materialism to Spiritualism. Well may Solomon say "There
is nothing new under the sun." Of course the Preacher
spoke of man, his hopes and fears, smiles and tears, sneers
and jeers, failings and hailings and wailings (like the " Water
of Lodore "), but not of mechanical inventions nor scientific
discoveries, which are progressive. Man always masticated,
but machines are only made. Hear Simon Kilham†:—

Theosophists (God and wisdom), a fanatical pest of philosophers,
who rose about the end of the 16th century, and made a figure in
almost every country in Europe. They pretended to derive all their
knowledge from divine illumination. They boasted that, by means of
this celestial light, they were not only admitted to the intimate knowledge of God, and of all divine truth, but had access to the most
sublime secrets of nature. They ascribed it to the singular manifesta-
tion of divine benevolence, that they were able to make such a use of
the element of fire, in the chemical art, as enabled them to discover
the essential principles of bodies, and to disclose stupendous mysteries
in the physical world. Hence they were also called " Fire Philosophers." They even pretended to acquaintance with those celestial
beings who form the medium of intercourse between God and man,

---

* *Sangre azul* (Spanish).

† Synoptically ; I have materially altered his title, but not a tittle of
his matter.

and to a power of obtaining from them, by the aid of magic, astrology, and other similar arts, various kinds of information and assistance. One of their chief leaders and ornaments was the celebrated Paracelsus, from whom they were also called Paracelsists. To this class also belonged Daniel Hoffman, Tok Böhme, Val Weigel, Swedenborg, Saint-Martin, Proli-Müller, &c. You may find a faint indication of it in that wicked " Sepher Toldos Jeschut," and in the " Paralipomena," commonly called the " Chronicles." And if it be true that by taking solated passages you can prove that every religion, every sect that has been, is, or has to be, can be countenanced by the Bible, why then there is a germ of truth in a——lie.

I (S.D.) opine that Theosophy is religion without its consolation, mysticism without its enlightenment, materialism without its science, deity without a Saviour. And this Mahatma re-incarnation, of what use is it in " being born again " at following terms of time if we cannot have, by experience of the past, something to guide us to the good in this present. However, this re-incarnation of the Theosophite seems to have had a credential echo in the minds of all thinkers in all ages. Pythagoras gravely asserted that he " remembered being an ass in a previous state of existence :" most people in our day forget that part of their former state ! ! The disciples asked the Saviour (John ix, 2) : " Master, who did sin, this man or his parents, that he was born blind ?" Now, if the punishment was for his parents' sins, it explains Exodus xx, 5, and Deut. v, 9 ; but if for his own, then *he* must have sinned before he was born. It does not follow that this was true, for Christ says (John ix, 13) : " Neither hath this man sinned, nor his parents ;" but it does follow that there was a current belief in a previous existence. Southey, in his " Doctor," gives some startling corroborations ; Sir Walter Scott mentions a remarkable case as occurring to himself at the funeral of the Princess Charlotte ; and the poet-painter Blake writes of something similar, which is generally termed the "knot." Most boys have read with delight the " Transmigrations of Indus," in which, through various stages, the hero is a man, then a snake, a fly, an elephant, and again a man. An American some years ago gave an opinion that man after death re-appeared on another planet in an improved state, and gradually developed into a higher being on successive spheres, attaining greater perfection through the illimitable orbs of the Astral System : and as space is immeasurable and time infinite, man's heaven would consist of this everlasting betterment in his condition—a kind of astronomical purgatory. The subject is boundless, and the finality is inenarrable. It was a mediæval idea that Christ descended into Hell (Sheol, not Gehenna) to visit the souls of men who were being purified until fit for heaven—and this was called the " Harrowing of Hell." Something like this was the condition of Hamlet's father, who was confined in fires till the foul deeds done in his days of youth were cleaned and purged away. This seems a sort of ultimate Universal Redemption, the very opposite to

The Benson family were from York, and related on the female side was Barry Cornwall*, whose real name was Waller Brian Proctor. His daughter is Adelaide Proctor, the poetess. Of the former family comes the present Archbishop of Canterbury : long may he wear the archi-episcopal mitre on his head.

Another Yorkshire celebrity was Thomas Jackson, the talented son of the Rev. Thomas Jackson, president of the Methodist Conference. This son was the first Principal of Battersea Training College, founded by Kay Shuttleworth and Carlton Tufnel about 1840, which was subsequently taken over by the National Society. From Battersea he was appointed Bishop-designate of Canterbury Settlement, in New Zealand ; but Bishop Selwyn objecting to the division of his diocese, Dr. Jackson returned to England, and became rector of Stoke Newington, where he died. He was a magnetic preacher ; and one of his sermons "The Cloke at Troas" (II. Tim., iv, 13) electrified the congregation at St. Michael's, Cornhill, where he had been invited to preach. A famous saying of his in pedagogy was : "Boys by listening learn, masters by talking teach." His work on the "Curiosities of the Pulpit"— droll, shrewd, solemn, and serious—is as readable as "Burton's Anatomy of Melancholy." He wrote also "Books on

---

an ineluctable and eternal damnation. I believe that all will be redeemed by the Saviour, irrespective of creed, sex, race, colour, class or caste. Now this general idea of pre-existence may arise thus : The brain is a limited liability company, in which two of the partners can and perhaps may act individually in an independent way of one another ; that while one is passant the other is couchant, as they say in heraldry. The cerebrum is the brainlet under the occiput, and the cerebrum the pulpy mass in the anterior of the cranium. Suppose one asleep, the other awake, and observing something taking place. This is called a reverie, day-dreaming, or being in a brown study (brown study is in French songer creux)—mere semi-consciousness, a lethargic comatose state. When the other faculty awakes, it receives a dull mental perception (of the past event) from the other faculty ; and this being doubled (as it were), the notion arises that the very fact that has just transpired happened just remotely. This dualism is a battle between the conscious self and the unconscious self awakened from the hypnotic state.

* Author of the "The Tragedy of Ion."

Animals," and a pamphlet on " Stoke Newington," a topo-
graphical review of historic personages and events connected
with that locality. Tolerant of all sects except the Roman
Catholic, against which he was as raging as a bull at a red
rag—he could praise Isaac Watts as the best hymn-writer
second to Charles Wesley. This was but natural in a
Churchman, son of a Methodist. Long will his memory
remain in our minds. His son, the Vicar of St. Bartholomew, in Moorfields, is the Rev. Blomfield Jackson, whose
godfather was Dr. Blomfield, whilom Bishop of London.

Tom Longbottom, of North Town End, was a queer
fellow : he once observed that, in a phrase of a certain
preacher, "the *felicity* of humanity," there was more expression than if he had said *happiness*. " Why," I replied,
" the words are synonymous." " Yes," he answered, " but
one is *more synonymous* than the other. On the occasion
of a man cutting his throat he told me "that the man's head
was almost severed from his body." Some one explained to
him that 'curious syllogism, II. Tim., iv., 13 : " One of
themselves, even a prophet of their own, said : 'The
Cretians are always liars.' Now if this be true, Epimenides
(the prophet St. Paul refers to) was also a liar : therefore it
was not true that the Cretians were liars. Consequently *he*,
Epimenides, was *not* a liar, and what he said was true," &c.,
&c., in a circle. To all this he merely rejoined : " Well
then, according to that, Epimenides was a *true liar*." To
one of his apprentices, who generally came late to his work,
but on this occasion was a little too soon, he remarked :
" Why, you used to be behind before, but you've come
early of late : it's fortunate you came to-day, or else you
would have found me within without." Someone asked him
if Mr. So-and-So had failed in business. He replied: "No;
his failure is due to his having failed to fail in business."
When in Sheepscar Street he——

ADDENDA.

No. 9. BLACK-CLOCK.   No. 173. LADY-BIRD. — The Scandinavian name for all beetles was *kluka*, and the lady-bird (though not a beetle) was also *lady-clock*. The water beetle *(Dytiscus marginalis)* was in an old Islandico-Latino-Danicum Lexicon, the *bruun-kluka;* and the common *scarabæus* in Old German was *chuleich* (pronounced with *k*). A gentleman from Bavaria says the *geotrupes stercorarius* is there called *kieleck*. In a funny way the Cockney pronounces the beetle "beedle," and many are the equivoques on beadle (a verger) and beedle (a beetle).

No. 52. FRATCH.—In my derivation of this word I am afraid I am faulty. At one time it was the fashion to derive all English words from the Latin; at another, from the French or German. Now, an Oxford Professor is making a run on the Sanskrit, forgetting that the old Indo-Germanic was as ancient as the Indo-Sanskrit. A lady of to-day connects lych-gate and Lichfield with the Scotch loch (a lake), ignoring that it refers to a *dead* body: Lichfield means a burial place, a churchyard, or, as the Anglo-Saxons termed it, God's-acre. This same lady in explaining Almondbury, refers it to a certain Almond and the Hebrew *Beriah*, meaning *sorrow*, because some Hebrew-speaking tribe *buried* him* there in *sorrow*. Another pertinently asks, "Who were the Hebrew-speaking tribes? When did they come to Yorkshire?" In response it is drily said that "Perhaps they were the lost Ten Tribes, who after the Babylonian Captivity wandered away and turned up in Yorkshire." In a facetious banter another remarks : "Some time ago I was afraid it was going to be proved that all our place-names were derived from the Greek ; now I feel equally alarmed at the thought that this lady intends to prove that they are all from the Hebrew."

---

* Almondbury ; no pun is meant or that would be punishment.

He further asks : " Cannot someone else shew that they are all from the Japanese ?" Such are the vagaries of philologists (word-hunters ?).

No. 70. BOGGARD.—In Portuguese *coco* is a bugbear or boggard. According to the Portuguese, De Barros, this word was applied to the fruit (afterwards called cocoa-nut) from its rude resemblance to a distorted human face, or a mask used by nurses to frighten refractory children ; but he shall speak for himself : " Esta casca tem huma maneira aguda, que quer semelhar o nariz posto entre dous olhos redondo."

I N D E X.

The numbers refer to paragraphs.

COLOPHON.

IF my style is discursive, it is also discoursive. There is a time to——(Eccles. iii.) The Avonian was sometimes an Autolycus, sometimes a Hamlet. The Low Moor ironworker shrewdly observed : " Aa can't al'ays be weäring me Sunday cloathes." Again, as the book was begun in 1866 and is finished now, in 1891, there is ample room for allowance. Asking for indulgence to my failings, and bidding my readers farewell,

I am, yours faithfully,

SAMUEL DYER.